ELIE WIESEL, A SURVIVOR OF AUSCH-WITZ, went to Russia to see for himself if the disturbing rumors of Soviet anti-Semitism were true. He was not prepared for what he found.

Jews in the streets of Moscow, Leningrad, Kiev were afraid to speak; informers filled their prayer houses; thousands of synagogues had been closed. Though they did not wear the yellow star, all their passports were stamped "JEW."

Three million Russian Jews live under a daily, silent fear imposed by Soviet discrimination and oppression. This unforgettable report tells what they suffer, and why they survive.

"A POWERFUL AND MOVING BOOK"
Walter Laqueur, *The New York Times*

Elie Wiesel was born in Hungary in 1928. After his liberation from Auschwitz, he made his way to Paris, where he began to write. Among other honors, Mr. Wiesel received the 1964 *Prix Rivarol* and the Jewish Heritage Award in 1966. He is the author of five novels: *Night, Dawn, The Accident, The Town Beyond the Wall,* and *The Gates of the Forest. The Jews of Silence* is his first work of historical reportage. Mr. Wiesel resides in New York City, where he is a correspondent for a leading Israeli newspaper.

Other **SIGNET** Books of Special Interest

THE JEWS
of SILENCE

ELIE WIESEL

*A Personal Report
on Soviet Jewry*

Translated from
the Hebrew with an Historical
Afterword by **NEAL KOZODOY**

A SIGNET BOOK from
NEW AMERICAN LIBRARY
TIMES MIRROR

Published in the United Kingdom by Valentine, Mitchell & Co. Ltd.

The Jews of Silence was originally written as a series of articles for the Israeli newspaper, Yediot Aharanot.
A portion of this book has appeared in the Saturday Evening Post.

Library of Congress Catalog Card Number: 66-21622

THIRD PRINTING

SIGNET TRADEMARK REG. U.S. PAT. OFF. AND FOREIGN COUNTRIES
REGISTERED TRADEMARK—MARCA REGISTRADA
HECHO EN CHICAGO, U.S.A.

SIGNET BOOKS are published by
The New American Library, Inc.,
1301 Avenue of the Americas, New York, New York 10019

FIRST PRINTING, NOVEMBER 1967

PRINTED IN THE UNITED STATES OF AMERICA

Contents

To the Reader

The pages that follow are the report of a witness. Nothing more and nothing else. Their purpose is to draw attention to a problem about which no one should remain unaware. However, they pose only the rudiments of a question, and reflect an anguish; they do not pretend to a solution or remedy.

Having never been involved in political action, I hope that what I have written here will neither exacerbate the cold war nor be used for political purposes. I have never engaged in propaganda, and have no intention of beginning now.

In the course of a trip to the Soviet Union that coincided with the Jewish High Holy Days of 1965, I tried to assess and, if possible, to penetrate the silence of the more than three million Soviet Jews who have, since the Revolution of 1917, lived apart from their people. Regarding other aspects of life in Russia, I do not feel qualified to pass judgment.

Clearly then I must emphasize that I have not attempted to create a work of literature or an authoritative political analysis. I wish only to add some impressions to the dossier. In doing so, I act as a witness, and my responsibilities are limited to those of a witness.

I went to Russia drawn by the silence of its Jews. I brought back their cry.

Elie Wiesel

June, 1966

*The
Jews
of
Silence*

1

Introduction

Their eyes—I must tell you about their eyes. I must begin with that, for their eyes precede all else, and everything is comprehended within them. The rest can wait. It will only confirm what you already know. But their eyes—their eyes flame with a kind of irreducible truth, which burns and is not consumed. Shamed into silence before them, you can only bow your head and accept the judgment. Your only wish now is to see the world as they do. A grown man, a man of wisdom and experience, you are suddenly impotent and terribly impoverished. Those eyes remind you of your childhood, your orphan state, cause you to lose all faith in the power of language. Those eyes negate the value of words; they dispose of the need for speech.

Since my return I have often been asked what I saw in the Soviet Union, what it was I found there. My answer is always the same: eyes. Only eyes, nothing else. Kolkhozi,* steel works, museums, theaters . . . nothing. Only eyes. Is that all? That is enough. I visited many cities, was shown what a tourist is shown, and have forgotten it all. But still the eyes which I cannot forget pursue me; there is no escaping them. Everything I have I would give them, as ransom for my soul.

I saw thousands, tens of thousands of eyes: in streets and hotels, subways, concert halls, in synagogues—especially in synagogues. Wherever I went they were waiting for me. At times it seemed as though the entire country was filled with nothing but eyes, as if somehow they had assembled there from every corner of the Diaspora, and out of ancient scrolls of agony.

All kinds of eyes, all shades and ages. Wide and narrow, lambent and piercing, somber, harassed. Jewish eyes, reflecting a strange unmediated Jewish reality, beyond the bounds of time and farther than the farthest distance.

* Singular, Kolkhoz: Soviet collective farm. Translator's Note.

Past or future, nothing eludes them; their gaze seems to apprehend the end of every living generation. God himself must surely possess eyes like these. Like them, He too awaits redemption.

If they could only speak . . . but they do speak. They cry out in a language of their own that compels understanding. What did I learn in Russia? A new language. That is all, and that is enough. It is a language easily learned in a day, at a single meeting, a single visit to a place where Jews assemble, a synagogue. The same eyes accost you in Moscow, and Kiev, in Leningrad, Vilna and Minsk, and in Tbilisi, the capital of the Georgian Republic. They all speak the same language, and the story they tell echoes in your mind like a horrible folk tale from days gone by.

For years I refused to believe it. Like many people, I was alive to the reports of Jewish suffering in Russia. I read all the books and articles and heard the testimony given at public meetings or behind closed doors. Yet I was unwilling, or unable, to believe it. I had too many questions, too many doubts and misgivings—not about the fact of Jewish suffering in the Soviet Union but about its scope. I was sure the reports were exaggerated. How else arouse public opinion; how else stir people from their apathy? I relied on my Jewish instinct, telling myself that if the situation were really so black I would of necessity believe it, without demanding proof. My own doubt was sign enough that the reports were exaggerated.

I was mindful, too, of the danger in drawing facile historical analogies between communist Russia and Europe under the Nazis. Even with regard to the Jewish problem, one is forbidden to make such comparisons. An abyss of blood separates Moscow from Berlin. The distance between them is not only one of geography and ideology; it is the distance between life and death.

If synagogues are being closed in Russia, I reasoned, Jews will simply go on praying in the ones that remain open. Are families prevented from reuniting? A new regime will soon come to power, and policy will change. Does the press conduct a campaign of anti-Semitism? Does it portray Jews as black marketeers, swindlers, drunkards? Does it disparage the state of Israel and malign the Zionist movement? This, too, will pass. Jews are accustomed to living in an unfriendly atmosphere. They have cultivated patience and humor, and they possess to a remarkable degree an understanding of their oppressors. Everything will pass; one must wait. The essential thing is that they be permitted to live, that their existence itself not be endangered, that there be no pogroms. And in Russia there are no pogroms; no one will dispute that. There are no detention camps. The situation, in other words, is not so unbearable.

Of course it could be better. Of course Jews in the free world are obliged to do everything in their power—to move heaven and earth—to see it improved. And of course one must exert pressure on the Kremlin to end discrimination and abolish the economic trials, whose victims were Jews. It is our duty to protest—and I too was among those who protested. But in several instances I was not at all certain whether the charges being leveled against the Soviets were not much too extreme and radical to be true.

I did not believe, for example, that the Russian government had embarked on a clear and relentless policy of "spiritual destruction." Despite, or because of what had happened in the recent past, I shrank from this idea, which for me will always remain in the exclusive domain of the German people. The Russians had fought against Hitler and in that fight had sacrificed twenty million lives. Of all people, they must know how impossible it is to "destroy" the spirit of a people—of any people. The very thought that they, or anyone, might even be attracted to such an idea struck me as anachronistic and absurd. One must, after all, learn *something* from history.

So I decided to go behind the Iron Curtain

to examine the situation with my own eyes. It was no longer possible for me to remain in New York or Tel Aviv and content myself with gestures of solidarity. The problem was too serious for compromises. If the protests were justified, they were in no way strong enough; if not, they had been much too strong. There was no other alternative. One is forbidden to play games with human lives.

In August I made my decision and set the departure date for early in September. I told my travel agent that I meant to spend the High Holy Days and Sukkot* in Russia, and gave him a list of the cities I intended to visit. It was necessary to make advance reservations for hotel rooms and flights between cities, but altogether the technical arrangements took no more than ten days, a minimum of bureaucratic activity. No red tape. Everything went simply and smoothly. The Russian government appears to welcome tourist dollars.

Other preparations proved more difficult. From everything I had read and heard, I knew that this was not to be a normal trip abroad. Over the years I had met more than a few people who had come back shattered by the experience. Something happens to the man whose travels bring him into contact with the Jews of Russia. Whether he goes on business

* Feast of Tabernacles (Deuteronomy 16, 13-16), an eight-day harvest festival celebrated in early fall. T.N.

or to see the Bolshoi Ballet, he soon forgets his original purpose and joins the stream. His life changes; the tourist becomes an apostle. And he leaves something of himself behind.

I was aware, then, that something would happen to me, but I did not know what; simply, I depended on its occurrence. I made no plans, I sought no contacts, I refused to arm myself with letters of introduction. I planned to wander about alone, and alone I would meet those I had come to see. I decided not to request personal interviews. I would stay away from official institutions and official spokesmen, visit neither the Foreign Ministry nor the Ministry of Religions. Political manifestos and worn-out promises did not interest me. I would not appear at the editorial offices of *Sovietish Heimland.* * Whatever Aron Vergelis* * and his comrades were prepared to tell me they had already repeated countless times before to visitors from the United States, France, and Israel. Nor did I intend to interview the rabbis or lay leaders of the various communities. Why place them in a difficult position? Why confuse them? I could observe their actions from afar.

I would approach Jews who held no position in society, who had never been placed in

* "Soviet Homeland"; a Yiddish magazine established in 1961, now a monthly. T.N.
** Editor of *Sovietish Heimland.* T.N.

the Soviet show window by Soviet authorities.
I was interested only in them and in what they
had to say. They alone, in their anonymity,
could describe the conditions under which they
live; they alone could tell whether the reports
I had heard were true or false—and whether
their children and their grandchildren, despite
everything, still wish to remain Jews. From
them I would learn what we must do to help
. . . or if they want our help at all. They
alone, I told myself, have the right to speak,
to advise, to demand. Theirs is the only voice
to which one is obliged to listen. My journey
to Russia would be a journey to find them.

I met one of them on my first evening in
Moscow, a few hours after my arrival from
New York and Paris. Actually, it was he who
found me, standing on the sidewalk in front
of the synagogue. From my clothes he could
tell I was foreign, and he asked me if I spoke
Yiddish. The darkness concealed his face. To
this day I have no idea whether the first Jew
who happened across my path on Russian soil
was a young rebel, impelled by stubborn bra-
vado and a Jewish conscience to risk serving
as a public spokesman, or an old man glutted
with fear who had finally decided, no matter
what the consequences, to break his silence.
I do not even know whether he was addressing

himself to me alone or through me to someone strange, abstract, and distant, who lived as a free man in a land drenched with sunlight and sea.

Why did he refuse to show his face? Perhaps he had none. Perhaps he had left it behind him somewhere in Siberia or, his crime unremembered, in the interrogation cell of a nameless prison. Perhaps he had given it away as a present to his enemies or to God. "Here, take it, I no longer need it. I have another, and it numbers three million."

Perhaps that was the reason he approached me stealthily and in shadow, while all around us thousands of shadows like his stood in the street and waited, powerless to say for whom or for what. Anxious lest I reveal him as a man without a face, he came wrapped in darkness, a simple Jew with no name and no particular destiny, a Jew identical to every other Jew in every city throughout that formidable land.

I heard only his voice, choked and fearful, a few tattered sentences whispered quickly in my ear, the simple gray words used by generations of Jews to describe their condition and fate: "Do you know what is happening to us?" He spoke for a few seconds. He wanted me to know. Finally came a request to remember everything and tell it all. "There is no time. We are nearing the end. Impossible to give you details. You must understand. If I am being watched, I will pay for this conversation. Do not forget."

I was excited and confused. It was too quick and unexpected. Yesterday I sat in New York joking with my friends. We laughed aloud. The transition was too sudden.

He continued to speak, alternating accusation with confession, demanding both justice and mercy at once. I wanted to press his hand, to promise him everything. I didn't dare. Maybe they were really watching us. A handshake could be costly. And so, unconsciously, I slipped into the reality of Jewish fear in Russia.

Suddenly he left me in the middle of a sentence, without saying good-by or waiting for my reaction. He disappeared into the living mass that crowded around the entrance to the synagogue.

I was to meet this Jew again, in Moscow and elsewhere. He always gave some sign by which I could recognize his presence. Once he thrust a note into my pocket; once he touched my arm without saying a word. Once I caught a secret wink of his eye. Each time I saw him he had changed his appearance. In Kiev I thought he was a construction worker, in Leningrad a civil engineer, in Tbilisi a university professor. But it was always he, for his story was the same and his request never varied. Do not forget; tell it all.

I left something of myself in that country, perhaps as a kind of collateral. Perhaps it was my eyes.

2

Fear

What are they afraid of? I don't know. Perhaps, afraid to ask, neither do they. I wasn't afraid to ask, but I never got an answer. Official government guides abruptly denied the existence of any such phenomenon, and the Western diplomatic observers whom I consulted simply said that the whole matter was an enigma to them. As for Jews, they smiled at me sadly. "You're an outsider. You wouldn't understand."

I cannot say, then, whether their fear is justified, but I know for a fact that it exists, and that its depths are greater than I had imagined possible. In city after city it confronted me like an impenetrable wall; on the other side, peering out of its own interstices, lurked only the final unknown.

Time after time, people with whom I had been talking slipped away without saying good-by or left me in the middle of a sentence. A person who had conversed with me one day denied knowing me the next. Once a technician who had arranged to meet me in the synagogue to give me particulars concerning a brother in Philadelphia never came. In Moscow I met a French Jew who told me he had come to Russia to visit a sister he had not seen since the war. When he arrived at her house in Lvov she refused to let him in. Later she appeared at his hotel and, in the five minutes she allowed herself to stay, begged him to leave the city, to go back to Moscow, or better, to France. "What did I do?" he cried. And I, to calm him, said, "Nothing. Try to understand, can't you? She's afraid." He began to shout. "Of whom? Of what?" I had no answer.

Perhaps there is none. Perhaps, in the absence of all objective correlatives, their dark and irrational fear exists simply as a thing in itself, without reason or purpose, serving no useful function, incapable of a reasoned justification. It exists because it exists, and it is therefore impossible to fight. No argument, no amount of careful rationalization can hope to unravel the nature of this fear, let alone dislodge its presence.

So far as anyone can tell, the years of terror are over. Stalin's maniacal hold on the country is a chapter in past history. During the last ten years something has *happened* in Russia; changes have taken place which cannot be lightly dismissed as the fictitious products of an efficient propaganda machine. The general populace is beginning to enjoy the benefits of society. Tensions have been noticeably alleviated. If you stop a man in the street, he will not hesitate to talk with you. The person in the airplane seat next to yours will join you in conversation, perhaps even tell jokes. From time to time you may meet an English-speaking citizen who will admit that the worker's homeland has yet to become a paradise on earth. Young people twisting in Russian night clubs would put San Franciscans to shame.

It is only the Jews then who live in permanent fear, in this infectious mystery. "Yes," one occasionally acknowledges, "times have changed, and for the better." But no explanation follows that remark.

"You wouldn't understand anyway."

It is true; I do not understand. Why are they so suspicious? Why do they behave like a community of terrorized captives, on the brink of some awful abyss? No one denies that the Jews have benefited from the recent easing of tension. Writers who had been liquidated or proscribed are now undergoing rehabilitation. Tens of thousands of Jews convicted of "Jewish nationalism" and sentenced to prison have been released. It is no longer dangerous to be known as a Yiddish writer; now and again one hears of whole evenings devoted to Yiddish songs and public readings of Yiddish works. A Yiddish magazine—never mind the quality of the writing—appears regularly each month. The legendary figure of Solomon Mikhoels* has been revived, and today even Ilya Ehrenburg** takes public pride in the fact that certain Jewish writers were among his closest friends.

Why are they afraid? I tried during my stay to ascertain precisely the consequence of boldness, but it was a futile effort. I badgered my hosts with questions. Is someone who speaks with a Jew from abroad thrown into prison? If you are seen strolling with a guest from America or Israel, will you be persecuted? One shred of evidence was all I required, a single example to convince me of the clear and present danger, of the imminence of some fatal blow. All my entreaties failed. "Do me

*Leading Yiddish actor and producer, murdered during the Stalin purges of 1949. T.N.

**b. 1891, Soviet Jewish author; one of a handful who survived the Stalin era. T.N.

a favor," one Jew told me, "don't ask simple questions." Another said, "If I told you, you wouldn't believe me. And even if you did you wouldn't understand."

I realized suddenly that there was no common language between us, that they persist in thinking in terms of "we" and "you." No wonder they refuse to speak to strangers; what's the use of talking? No matter what one says, the meaning is lost. Fear has created a language of its own, and only one who lives with it day after day can ever hope to master the intricacies of its syntax.

I did, however, succeed in discovering the answer to one riddle . . . not *what* they fear, but whom: Informers, Jewish agents of the secret police who attend synagogue to observe the behavior of their fellow Jews. They have eyes to see, ears to hear, hands to write. You must always know who stands behind you, as you know beyond doubt before whom you will be called to render your accounts.

At first I refused to believe this. The idea of Jews informing on Jews was too repellent, especially in the House of God. But they believe it. Any number of times—in Moscow, in Leningrad, and particularly in Kiev—I was cautioned by a wink or a low whisper, "Watch out for that one; he works for *them*." Their suspicion can reach the pitch of terror. No one trusts anyone. A Jew profoundly immersed in prayer is pointed out as a fake, a government agent, worshiping not the God of Israel but his enemies. "But how do you know that?" I found myself protesting. "Mightn't you be slandering an honest man for no good reason?"

"Are you telling *us* what is right and what is not?" Their gaze moves between grief and derision. "Do you mean to instruct *us* in matters of guilt and innocence?" Wounded and ashamed, one can only keep silent before such outbursts. Whether their suspicions are founded on fact or not is clearly unimportant. *They* regard them as factual, and their conviction only serves to compound the fear in which they live.

Occasionally I was a witness to incidents that would have seemed funny or absurd had they not been so tragic. "Do you see that redhead," someone would whisper in my ear, "sitting in the third row, pretending to pray with all his might? Keep away from him; he's one of theirs." Not an hour later the redhead himself would approach with lowered voice. "The Jew you were talking with before . . . we know him. He works for them."

You cannot understand these Jews and that, more than anything else, is what shocks you so. Holidays and Sabbaths, when you see them standing outside or gathered in the synagogue, they look oppressed and poor; they seem to be walking, bent over, through a world of the dead, their eyes reflecting sad and distant mysteries. You pity them. Somehow you understand their sadness. Their sadness, but not their fear. I found myself trembling as I asked what had happened to create this wall between us, what it was that prevented me from comprehending in the slightest degree the reason for their fear. Am I not a Jew like them? Are we not brothers in the same ancient tradition, sharing a common belief in the eternity of Israel? Do we not observe together the commandment bidding us to sanctify our lives? That such a gap should stretch between us seems impossible. Yet, apparently, everything is possible. Fear remains the one point of contact that binds us to one another, but we stand on opposing sides of the line, facing each other. All I can do is pray that my pain reaches out to them, as their fear reaches out to touch me.

If, driven by fear, they were to erupt in communal hysteria, I would feel less pain. If they screamed, wept, succumbed to a mass nervous breakdown, I would know how to react, what to do . . . especially what to think. Analogies would come to mind from recent Jewish history or from the period of the Russian pogroms. But there is nothing in the history of the Jewish people to compare with this enclosed and silent fear. Perhaps it follows its own rules, perhaps not. Perhaps it follows no rules whatsoever but instead denies all logic and escapes all human understanding. Such fear, in its absolute power, can descend only upon those suffering from an overwhelming sense of persecution. Shut off from help, its victims are swiftly brought to the edge of despair, where devoid of hope they await the end.

The situation does on rare occasion reach the level of a larger delusion. On "Kol Nidrei"• night two young Russians hurled a rock through a window of the Moscow synagogue. They may have been drunk, or simply malicious. In any event the incident was quickly over. No one got excited. But the next morning, in a second synagogue, it was rumored that a serious clash had broken out between the Jews and their attackers.

A similar story came to my attention in Tbilisi, where I was approached one night on a side street by two Jews who asked me to tell everyone I saw about the "terrible things" that had occurred a few days before in Kotaisi, a town about four hundred kilometers away. What had happened? Riots, bloodshed. A number of Jews had been injured, a few imprisoned. I looked into the matter; it was all a lie. No one had been injured, no one imprisoned.

•Prayer for remission of vows and oaths, chanted on the eve of Yom Kippur. T.N.

Why was I misinformed? One person I asked suggested that the two were informers who meant to mislead me into spreading false reports. Another said they were good men who had simply spoken out of fear, embellishing what they had heard with details of their own imagining. They had acted under the influence of that mass paranoia which from time to time attacks the Russian Jewish community.

My first encounter with that community and with the fear that pervades it took place on the night I arrived in Russia. It was Yom Kippur* eve, and as I stood in the Great Synagogue of Moscow, I thought I had come to pray in the company of Marannos,** Jews who once each year decided to leave their places of hiding and worship their Creator in public. I felt like a stranger, a gentile, among them.

Yet, on the surface at least, I might have been in any prewar synagogue in Europe or America, not in the very heart of the Russian

---

* Day of Atonement, the most solemn day of the Jewish year, culmination of the Ten Days of Repentance begun on New Year's Day, Rosh HaShanah. Jews traditionally observe a twenty-four-hour fast on Yom Kippur. T.N.

** Specifically, Spanish and Portuguese Jews who openly professed Christianity during and after the medieval Inquisition but continued to practice Judaism in private; hence, "secret Jews." T.N.

capital, ten minutes away from the golden domes of the Kremlin and from the infamous "Lublianka," headquarters of the secret service, its darkened cellars once the final home of many who were tortured and condemned to die simply because they were Jews.

The sanctuary was brightly lit and crowded. Many were wearing white holiday robes and prayer shawls. As usual the number of older people was large, but there were also many of middle age and quite a few between the ages of twenty and thirty. Three generations had come together—grandfather, who still remembered the edicts of the Czar; his son, who had spent years in a labor camp in Siberia; and his grandson . . . but what was he doing here? Someone, a comrade at school or at work, must have reminded him that after all he, too, was a Jew, only a Jew—by force if not by choice.

The old people prayed with all their hearts, the younger generation sat listening in silence. They seemed thoughtful, worried, distracted. But this was only natural; it was Yom Kippur, the Day of Judgment. Who shall live and who shall die, who shall be banished and who set free, who shall be afflicted and who shall be at rest. Thoughts like these occupy the mind of every Jew on this night, wherever he may be. But here they are of immediate moment.

The prayers went on in an orderly fashion,

with traditional melodies sung by a cantor and choir. The scrolls of the Tórah* were removed from the ark, and as the procession wound around the pulpit the elderly rabbi, Yehuda-Leib Levin, declared in a trembling voice, "*Or zarua la-tzaddik* . . . Light is sown for the righteous, and gladness for the pure of heart." What light? What gladness? The cantor sang "Kol Nidrei." Here and there one heard a quiet sigh. A woman sobbed. And as the final blessing was intoned, "Blessed art Thou who hast kept us alive, and hast sustained us, and enabled us to reach this day," a shudder passed through the congregation. Another year.

Suddenly I sensed my neighbors eying me peculiarly. Their look was unfriendly, insulting. They were examining me, trying to tear an imaginary mask from my face and thus reveal the true purpose of my presence among them. I heard whispers. "Does anyone know him? No one. "Does anyone know where he's from or why he's here?" No one knew. No one could possibly know. I had spoken to no one, had in fact just arrived, almost directly from the airport. Barely seven hours before I had been in Paris.

Their suspicion did not surprise me, although it did trouble me somewhat. I tried

---

* The Pentateuch, or Five Books of Moses. T.N.

to start a conversation; they pretended not to hear. The fact that I had deliberately chosen to sit in the main part of the synagogue instead of in the visitors' section only increased their mistrust. When I spoke, they pretended not to understand Yiddish. Despite the crowding and the close quarters, a kind of distance opened between us.

It was only when I began to pray aloud, in witless desperation, that the barriers fell. The Prince of Prayer had come to my aid. They listened closely, then drew nearer; their hearts opened. They crowded around me. The crush was unbearable, but I loved it. And the questions poured out. Are there Jews in America? In Western Europe? Are they well off? Any news from Israel? Can it resist its enemies? All they wanted was to hear me talk. They refused to answer my questions. "Better not ask," said one. Another said the same. "We can't say, we can't talk," said a third. Why not? "Because. It's dangerous." They turned to me with hunted looks. I could never be one of them, because I would never be in their place. The wall of fear had risen to cut us off.

"Don't talk," one said to me. "Just pray. That is enough. How good it is to know there are young Jews in the world who still know how to pray." I felt like an outsider, a sinner. . . .

I forgot the rabbi and the cantor and the

choir. Even God receded from my mind. I closed my eyes and raised my voice in prayer. Never in my life have I prayed with such a sense of devotion.

3

A Gift

"Masters mine, the Holy Presence dwells not among the sad of heart!" The old man was shouting, a strange fire gleaming in his deep eyes. " '*V'samahta b'hagecha!*—And thou shalt rejoice in thy festivals!' A command from the Torah, my masters, a commandment we fulfill at its proper time, no matter where we may be. Today is our festival, the festival of Sukkot—let it be so! I demand the holiday air, for the heavens have decreed that today we rejoice. Too difficult, my masters? Let it be seven times difficult, no one will dampen our joy. We alone determine when to rejoice, when to accept our affliction in love and in silence. What, does it require skill to dance when the heart is glad? No, no, I say just because we cannot raise our heads we must make

manifest our gladness, we must utter song with
all our being! You have heard me, my masters?
Have you understood? If there is no joy, let
us create it from nothing, and bestow it as a
holiday gift upon our Lord!"

I was in a small Sukkah* somewhere in Leningrad. About a hundred *hasidim*** had
pushed their way in to hear an old Jew, his
face glowing and his heart raging with heat,
his aristocratic features giving transient bodily
form to the angel of hope. Everything he
touched took fire. When you shook his hand,
you felt strengthened and purified . . . pro-
tected.

I couldn't take my eyes away from him. I
heard that there were *hasidim* in Russia, but
not like him. I watched him in wonder: A
Jew who refused absolutely to submit. Such
Jews had celebrated the festivals of Israel in
the concentration camps of Europe, in the
shadow of the ovens.

The old man spoke. "Moshe! I request you,
Moshe, sing us a tune."

Moshe was embarrassed. Unlike the old

---

*Booth or tabernacle, hung with fruit of the harvest;
commemorates years when Jews lived in huts in the wil-
derness. T.N.

**Adherents of Hasidism, a form of orthodox Judaism
that stresses enthusiastic piety. When first established by
the Baal Shem Tov in the eighteenth century Hasidism
defined itself in opposition to the rigid legalism of much
Eastern European orthodoxy. T.N.

man, who wore a black *kapota*,* Moshe was dressed in a heavy coat. He was evidently a laborer or low-ranking bureaucrat who had somehow managed to take the day off. An observant Jew, he would stay home tomorrow, too, to celebrate the second day of Sukkot. He would come here to pray, to join his companions in song, and to forget. But he would not sing alone. Perhaps his embarrassment was a result of his not wearing a beard or not having a black *kapota* like the old man.

"I want you to sing." This time it came as a command. "I want our guest to tell the Jews of the world that in Leningrad we know how to sing! Did you hear, Moshe? They must know!"

"Yes, but . . ."

"No buts; not today. The rest of the year is for buts. Not on a holiday, Moshe, not in the Sukkah, not in the presence of a guest from across the sea. Let him be the one to say but. Let him go home and report that the Jews of Russia live under such and such conditions, *but* they still know how to sing."

"What shall I sing?" Moshe's voice took on the tone of an obedient child.

"You know. The Yiddish song I love so. But slowly now, don't hurry it. Slow and gentle, so we hear every word, every note. . . ."

Moshe closed his eyes and began to sing

---

*Black robe worn by *hasidim*. T.N.

something in Yiddish, an old tune about a young Jewish boy who went to Heder* and did not want to learn Torah. Now he has a new master, a dog named Balak, who speaks a different language and teaches a different law. But then the young man returns to the days of his childhood. Is it too late? No, the *rebbe*** still waits for him. The song was a simple one, a song of experience, its symbolism and its moral transparently clear. Moshe sang and the old man wept. "Again," he begged him. Moshe began again, afraid to disobey. And the old man continued to weep. "Again, Moshe, again!" Five times, twelve times. The old man wept in silence, holding his breath, as if hoping the song would change, would achieve by repetition a different ending. Disappointed, his tears flowed down into his beard.

Hoarse with the effort, Moshe's voice became weaker and weaker until his strength left him altogether. He finished the refrain of the last stanza and stopped. No one moved; nobody uttered a sound as a heavy silence crept over the room. It was as if they feared to revive the present. Even the old one seemed to have become calmer, seemed to be dream-

---

* Jewish elementary school. T.N.

** Yiddish diminutive of Hebrew *rav*, used primarily to designate a Hasidic rabbi. T.N.

ing a distant dream, listening perhaps to a new song, or an old one, from a new world or an old. He may even have entered the Temple of Melody, where now he rested, satisfied.

Suddenly he awoke with a start. "What's happened to you all? Silent again? We must not submit, I tell you! I order you to rejoice, I command you to create a disturbance! A tabernacle in the desert, is that what you say? I want to see a tabernacle within a tabernacle! A festival within a festival! Well, masters mine, what do you say? My good friends, what are you waiting for? Shame! We have a guest, do we not? A guest from across the sea, a messenger! Is this our gift to our brothers? No! I tell you, no! A song of gladness for our guest, let him tell of the gladness in our hearts! Do you hear? I tell you . . ."

The sentence unfinished, his head fell forward on his chest and he sobbed like a child.

I stayed with them for a few hours, and I admit I envied them. Where did they get their prodigious courage, where did they find, how did they ever preserve, the hidden power of their faith? What great and terrible mystery has prevented their complete disintegration? Certainly the degree to which they have suffered and the nature of their torment far exceed our own experience. We suffered at the hands of the Nazis, but their oppressors are of a different breed entirely, one apparently devoted to a pure and humane ideology. The tortures inflicted upon us were brought to an end somehow, while they remain caught in an unending ring of terror.

Think a minute. Who were the first, the principal victims of the pogroms? They were. The first to be eliminated in the communist purges of the thirties. And the first to be murdered by the invading Germans. These first, hundreds of thousands of Jews, old men, women, and children, in the Ukraine and White Russia, from Minsk to Kiev, from Lvov to Vilna. Murdered or thrown alive into mass graves, long before the ovens of Auschwitz began to cover heaven and earth with human ashes. And in Stalin's last years, who were the victims of his mad liquidation programs? They were. The first to be victimized, the last to be redeemed.

Years pass, governments change, patterns of life are altered. But for them, only for them, nothing changes. Or almost nothing. Our nightmare, somehow, was buried; not theirs. Somehow we have grown accustomed to living in abundance and freedom, even in luxury, but especially in freedom. And they? They have grown accustomed to their fear.

Still they have not yielded to despair. In spite of everything, they sing, and they think of us, the Jews outside. They are alone in their battle; yet in their attempts to overcome isolation and terror they work not only for themselves , but for us. For our sake they sing, and to us alone they present this gift of their own making.

I sat with them through their holiday "banquet." Bread, fish, and homemade wine. Nobody missed the meat, and we did nicely without other delicacies. I don't know precisely how, but the Jews sitting around me in that Sukkah managed in some way to overcome their melancholy. They grew flushed and lively, began to tell jokes; it was as if they had just liberated themselves from the dark threat that pursued them. They began to sing, louder and louder; despite the narrow quarters a few began to dance. "O purify our hearts to serve Thee in truth." They accented *truth*. And for that, too, I envied them.

So as not to insult them, I did my best to participate in their happiness. I drank the wine they offered me, ate the bread they sliced especially for me, joined them in their singing. But I was unable to rid myself of the depression that had overcome my spirit. As if in a dream I asked myself over and over, "Why them and not me?" No answer. I knew that tomorrow I would be leaving and they would stay. I promised myself not to forget them—at any rate, not quickly—but I knew already that no matter how I told their story or how much I might try to help them, I could never fulfill my obligation.

"You will tell the Jews outside that you saw us dancing?" The old man's face radiated pride, or perhaps an excess of pain.

"I will tell them."

"And that you heard us singing?"

"I will."

"And were a witness to our rejoicing? You will tell them how we fulfilled the command-ment of joy?"

"I will tell them, yes."

Except, I am not sure we deserve their gift, or their joy. Or this story.

They did not complain, they didn't criticize the regime or lament the hard conditions of their lives. It was from other sources that I learned of that, and of the attempts being made to annihilate the Jewish soul by eradicat-ing all memory of its historical identity. Of all this I was informed in other circles, where I learned too that contrary to well-placed rumor, Gedaliah Pecharsky* was still in prison, that Leningrad, too, has its share of informers, and that it is impossible to combat the assimila-tion being forced on Jewish youth. There is simply no one to teach young children the

*Lay leader of Leningrad Jewish community, arrested and sentenced to prison in 1961 on charges of espionage. T.N.

Hebrew alphabet. Many are not even circumcised. The ornate room in the local synagogue which was meant for wedding ceremonies is rarely used for that purpose anymore. There are three hundred thousand Jews in Leningrad but less than ten weddings a year in the synagogue, and no more than five Bar Mitzvah celebrations. "And the situation here is considered good. At least," one told me, "I can die as a Jew. In Moscow there is no longer a Jewish cemetery."

The *hasidim* do not talk; they only sing. But their song comes up from a great depth to smash your heart. In their presence you feel moved to emulate them. Not for their sake, but for your own.

I met them in Moscow, too, and Kiev. They are associated with various *hasidic* houses, not just the Lubavitch. And they all pray in the same synagogue, indeed in the same room, each group according to its own liturgical formulas. Standing in the prayer hall you hear the Karlin version with one ear and the Bratzlaver with the other. Yet their hearts are united in true brotherhood. You find no trace of the dissensions that plague most *hasidic* houses, rather an infinite and uninhibited love of Israel, a pure solidarity of spirit, and a sanctity which *hasidic* leaders in Jerusalem or Williamsburg would do well to study.

How many of them are there? No more than a few thousand, scattered throughout the country, most in large cities. Their children grow up in a Jewish atmosphere and receive a traditional education. Some of them wear earlocks, and I saw a number of young men with beards. They gather in a private home to study Talmud. On Sabbath they attend a lecture on the Bible, and during long winter evenings they tell *hasidic* wonder tales, passed on from generation to generation like an underground Oral Law.

What about observance, I asked one of them, certain he would tell me that in light of extenuating circumstances (which one need not go into) it had become necessary to adopt a more lenient attitude toward the commandments. Not at all. On the contrary, he had become stricter than ever in his observance, stricter than Jews elsewhere. His children, for instance, stayed home from school on the Sabbath, although he knew that the consequences were likely to be unpleasant. But there was no alternative, he told me. Perhaps God will take pity; if not, not. His children might suffer, but they will not have desecrated the Sabbath. I quoted him the law: preservation of life supersedes observance of the Sabbath. Not here, he replied. Once we forfeit this commandment, or another iike it, the next step is to forfeit all of them. Better not begin in that direction.

How they have managed to live by their sacred tradition, without books, without outside help or encouragement, without the hope of a new generation, is a mystery to me. What supports them? How do they overcome the threat of a petrifying rigidity on the one hand and onrushing assimilation on the other? What hidden forces operate among them? It is all a riddle. The prophet Elijah, the rabbis say, will answer all questions when he comes. But let him come soon, while there are Jews in Russia who still await him, and who will be able to recognize him. If he delays much longer, it may be too late—not only for them, but for us.

4

Babi Yar

Kiev brings to mind Babi Yar. Kiev *is* Babi Yar. Not that Kiev is not beautiful—it is enchanting. A splendid landscape, parks and palaces, ancient churches and museums, hotels and restaurants, green hills, mountains, and the Dnieper River . . . a tourist's paradise.

But for the Jewish tourist there is only one point of interest in the capital city of the Ukraine, an attraction missing on the map and excluded from guided tours: Babi Yar. Wherever you are taken you cannot escape the feeling that something, the essential thing, is being concealed—the hundreds of thousands of murdered souls who made this metropolis a city of horror. Finally the realization comes that there is really no need for you to be shown that spot, where in the year 1941 be-

tween Rosh HaShanah * and Yom Kippur who
knows how many Jews were buried, dead or
alive. The government guides are right; there
is no reason to go there, there is nothing to
see at Babi Yar. You can see it downtown, in
every square and on every street; nothing and
everything. All you need is a bit of imagina-
tion, and, breaking through the surface, you
can then identify Babi Yar with the figure of
Bogdan Chmielnitzki, ** the man who pre-
figured it, who prepared the way, the man
who made Babi Yar possible.

The Ukrainian prides himself on his wars
against foreign invaders. Bogdan Chmielnitzki
is the national hero of the Ukraine, the same
Chmielnitzki who murdered Jews in 1648 and
1649, slaughtering women, children, and old
men and destroying defenseless Jewish communities. But this is a small point, it hardly
detracts from his heroism. The statues erected
in Kiev and elsewhere to perpetuate the memory and example of Chmielnitzki are not intended to commemorate those particular epi-
sodes of his life. Did he kill Jews—so what?
Hardly a terrible thing, and in any case a thing
of the past. Ukrainians are quick to forgive
sins of that sort. And if the Jews refuse to

* Jewish New Year. T.N.

** Cossack chieftain; in 1648 led an insurrection against
the Polish and Ukrainian gentry that resulted in the
massacre of numerous Jewish communities. T.N.

forget, that is their business. The Ukrainian sense of reality is more highly developed. Out of esteem for Chmielnitzki they also forget Babi Yar.

As a warrior who hoped to lead his people to independence by the sword, Chmielnitzki failed. But as a murderer of Jews he was successful. The story of Babi Yar will be recorded as his greatest victory.

How many Jews were killed at Babi Yar? Exact estimates are hard to come by. Some say seventy thousand, others a hundred and fifty thousand. Unlike those in Auschwitz, the Germans and their local collaborators here did not bother with statistics . . . perhaps because Ukrainians have no head for figures.

Eyewitnesses say that for months after the killings the ground continued to spurt geysers of blood. One was always treading on corpses. Only recently someone dug up a new mass grave, and it is generally held that this was not the last. So it is impossible to rely on figures; the dead themselves ensure the need for occasional revisions of former estimates.

Non-Jews in Kiev do not like to talk about Babi Yar. Even the quasi-official spokesmen of the Jewish community prefer to pass over it in silence rather than admit the simple, cruel, incriminating fact that the general populace of Kiev, including faithful members of the Communist Party, did not lift a finger to prevent the mass murders. The citizenry saw it all, knew it all and remained silent. No one raised a voice in protest; not a single tear was shed. Stores remained open; life went on as usual. Many of those who lived in Kiev during those days are still there today. Who knows, a few of them might even occupy important municipal positions. Surely it is preferable not to linger over a subject which is far too delicate and far too dangerous to discuss. It is a little like walking over a mine field.

Indeed, those who are prepared to speak the whole truth about Babi Yar can find no one to listen. I was told, for instance, about a woman who rose from her grave in that ravine of death. She had only been wounded. At night she managed to extricate herself from the tangle of bodies that had fallen on top of her and fled, naked. She was given shelter by a Ukrainian. The next day he turned her over to the Germans. Once again she was forced into the long lines, stripped of her clothes, and shot. Once again she was saved, and this time managed to escape. But her mind had snapped. Now she rants aloud, remembering forgotten things, and people say, "Poor woman, she lives in another world."

A second woman was pointed out to me in the synagogue. She, too, lives in another world, but she was not among those taken out to be shot. She had managed to hide and escape.

Her husband, a ritual butcher and a scholar, was caught and killed with the others. After the liberation, his widow somehow received a long letter he had left for her. She shut herself in her room and for three days and three nights read the letter, over and over, hundreds of times, line by line and word by word. Then she went to Babi Yar and called to her husband in a loud voice. The next day she did the same. Now this is all she does, every day of the year, except for Sabbath and holidays. She doesn't talk to other people, doesn't pay visits to friends or gossip with her neighbors. Whatever she has to say is written in that letter. Everything she has to say she screams out loud at Babi Yar. The dead listen to her. Only the dead.

There is nothing to see, then, at Babi Yar. And whoever goes to see will understand that there is nothing to be seen. Then he will go out of his mind with the shock.

I was in Kiev on the second day of Sukkot. The Jews I found in the synagogue differed from those in other cities. Their fear is more solid, more compact, and perhaps more justified. Their own leaders terrorize them . . . you can feel it in your bones. Nowhere else in Russia did I see such hatred on the part of Jews toward their own leaders.

No sooner had I entered the synagogue—

during the occupation it had served as a stable for the German army—when two men appeared at my side to offer me a seat up front in the section reserved for guests. I declined, explaining that I was ready to forgo the honor, being neither a rabbi nor a rabbi's son, and that I preferred worshiping together with the common people. The two had not been endowed with a sense of humor. They issued an ultimatum: either I conform to custom and obey their request or go home. They were not in the least reluctant to cause a scene. There had already been a number of cases in which guests were thrown out of the synagogue for being too stubborn. Since I had no choice, I thanked my hosts for their gracious welcome and let them lead me captive to the isolated bench in the front of the hall.

The *gabbai** of the synagogue was a clumsy and vulgar Jew by the name of Jonah Gandelman. His eyes were permanently enraged, his voice continually shouting. He had the domineering character of a military commander and seemed to hold a whip over the congregation. One look from him, and the object of his wrath was cowed into obedience.

What had prompted a man like this, a Jew who had studied Torah in his youth, to seek out this hated role? A lust for power?

*Lay leader of Jewish community. T.N.

A need for respect? Or was he perhaps aiming to safeguard the general good, thinking he could help his fellow Jews by standing between them and the outside world?

Whatever the reason, he used all the means at his disposal—and they were many and terrible—to separate the worshipers not so much from the government as from the guests who were drawn to the synagogue on Sabbaths and holidays. From where he stood on the pulpit, supervising his flock, he would unabashedly interrupt the service to revile anyone who had dared to give a surreptitious wink in the direction of the visitors' bench.

He did not speak to me. That task had been delegated to his aides who surrounded me on all sides and described to me the state of the Jews in their city. The news was all good. Anti-Semitism in Kiev? God forbid. There were, here and there, a few fanatic Jew haters, but the government was taking proper care of them. What about the poisonous books of Professor Kichko (such as *Judaism without Embellishment*)? Banned from the market. Of course the whole affair was unfortunate, especially since it was a member of the Academy who wrote such lies and the book was printed by a government press and distributed in tens of thousands of copies by an official government agency. It proves that something was rotten, certainly, but what can you do . . . a thing like that can happen anywhere. The important thing is that the book was suppressed, the damage repaired. The Jews have it very good here. They live in absolute freedom, in wealth and abundance, God be praised. Why is there only one synagogue? The Jews are to blame; they have forgotten their religion. And no Jewish school? The youth is at fault; they are not interested in Judaism. And why was the baking of matzah* prohibited for the last couple of years? The ovens were to blame; they didn't conform to health standards. New ones are being built; this year everyone will eat matzah. In general there is no cause for alarm. Whoever wishes to live a Jewish life in Kiev may do so. If you want to eat kosher meat, there are twenty ritual butchers in the neighborhood; take your pick. And *mohalim?* ** Enough, and more. But the parents are to blame; they want nothing to do with their people. Weddings? Of course, only they are civil ceremonies; the couples are at fault. Is there a rabbi? Naturally, but he is ill. He is much too old. Is there no one else, will there ever be anyone else to take his place? No. The Jews are at fault.

The Jews sang praises to the God of Israel,

---

* Unleavened bread eaten by religious Jews during the holiday of Passover. T.N.

** Singular, *mohel:* Ritual circumcisor. T.N.

the *kohanim** blessed the people of Israel, and the *gabbai's* aides continued to perform their sole function, indicting the children of Israel.

In spite of all this, I established contact with one of the worshipers through a monologue of admonition and bitter testimony. Even as my hosts were doing their best to take my mind off the congregation, I suddenly heard someone chanting an unfamiliar prayer, a prayer not to be found in the Sukkot liturgy. He stood three rows behind me, an elderly man, rather tall, his face suffused with an uncommon purity of expression. He was profoundly immersed in prayer, but mingled in his devotions were snatches of prose intended for my ears alone. "Thou hast chosen us from among all nations . . . don't believe them . . . Thou hast loved us and taken pleasure in us . . . they do not speak for us, they work against us . . . and because of our sins we were exiled from our land . . . know that it is bad for us here, that we are nearing the end . . ."

Thus I received a detailed account of Jewish life in Kiev. Anyone who teaches his children Torah takes a dreadful risk. One who talks to a guest from abroad is reprimanded. They no longer imprison new offenders, but those

---

* Members of priestly class, as distinct from "Levites" and "Israelites." Traditionally, descendants of Aaron the High Priest. T.N.

incarcerated two years ago for the crime of "Jewish nationalism" have yet to be released. Jews are haunted by a relentless insecurity, afraid to speak Yiddish in the street, afraid to approach the government or even their own leaders with religious requests. Anti-Semitism is common among the general populace; Jews are made to suffer from it, but it is forbidden to talk, forbidden to complain. Who knows what the day will bring? The Jewish spirit is deteriorating rapidly; it cannot hold out much longer.

The old Jew prayed on, less to God than to me. All the time he seemed to be reading his report out of the prayer book in his hands. It was he, and not the cantor, who served that day as spokesman for the Jewish community, requesting intercession from above.

I spent three full days in Kiev without finding anyone who would take me to Babi Yar. Everyone had an excuse. The Intourist guides were too busy. Jews who had managed to elude my bodyguards and speak with me briefly did not dare to be seen in my company for any length of time. Jonah Gandelman's aides claimed that the question should be taken up with the Office of Tourism, not with them.

Finally I remembered the advice of a Western diplomat I had met in Moscow; I hired a taxi. I gave the driver twenty rubles—a week's salary—and told him, "Babi Yar." He understood immediately and smiled. It was only later that the suspicion arose in my mind that his smile may have been more mocking than friendly.

We traversed the city, passing through the Podol quarter and stopping a moment near the old cemetery. Then we continued for another two kilometers until we reached a broad, open area. In the distance were new housing developments. On my right a new highway, on my left a construction site. "Babi Yar," the driver shrugged his shoulders, as if to explain, *You can see with your own eyes there's nothing here.* He was right. You have to close your eyes to see the thousands falling into an open grave. You have to concentrate with all your energy to hear their cries in this silence which seems so restful and so natural. Where are the mass graves? Where is the blood? Does anything visible remain of that drama of horror? Nothing. Blue skies, a long smooth road, the movement of traffic. And the driver's smile. I stayed there for an hour, my feet glued to the ground, searching for a sign, a memorial of some kind. Nothing. There is nothing to see at Babi Yar.

We returned to the hotel, and I continued on my travels. About a week later I was back in Moscow, where I met with a number of friends in the Western diplomatic corps. One of them told me that the same thing had happened to him. No one would show him Babi Yar, and he, too, wound up hiring a cab. But he was not at all sure that the driver had taken him to the right place; maybe they had gone somewhere else. Presumably that is a common practice in Kiev.

Only then did it occur to me that my driver might have led me astray as well. How could I be sure we had gone to Babi Yar? I remembered his deceitful smile. There was no doubt in my mind now; he had cheated me, had brought me to the wrong spot. My disappointment lasted no more than a minute. Against his wishes the driver had shown me something that I had unconsciously been aware of for some time. Thanks to him and to his deceit, I was finally able to understand that Babi Yar is not a geographical location. Babi Yar is not in Kiev, no. Babi Yar *is* Kiev. It is the entire Ukraine. And that is all one needs to see there.

5

Celebration in Moscow

Where did they all come from? Who sent them here? How did they know it was to be tonight, tonight on Arkhipova Street near the Great Synagogue? Who told them that tens of thousands of boys and girls would gather here to sing and dance and rejoice in the joy of the Torah? They who barely know each other and know even less of Judaism—how did they know that?

I spent hours among them, dazed and excited, agitated by an ancient dream. I forgot the depression that had been building up over the past weeks. I forgot everything except the present and the future. I have seldom felt so proud, so happy, so optimistic. The purest light is born in darkness. Here there is darkness; here there will be light. There must be—it has already begun to burn.

From group to group, from one discussion to the next, from song to song, I walked about, sharing with them a great celebration of victory. I wanted to laugh, to laugh as I have never done before. To hell with the fears of yesterday, to hell with the dread of tomorrow. We have already triumphed.

He who has not witnessed the Rejoicing of the Law in Moscow has never in his life witnessed joy. Had I come to Russia for that alone, it would have been enough.

It had snowed the week before. The day before, it rained. My friends in the diplomatic corps made no attempt to conceal their anxiety. Bad weather would ruin the holiday. Snow—that was all right. But we prayed to Him-who-causeth-the-wind-to-blow-and-the-rain-to-fall to postpone His blessing. For His sake, if not for ours, and for the sake of those who had waited all year long for this night, for this chance to prove that they are mindful of their origins, are mindful of Mount Sinai and their people.

The "festival of youth" has become something of a Russian tradition since it first began four or five years ago during the period of internal easement inaugurated by Nikita Khrushchev. At first the festivals were attended by a few hundred students; then the number grew into the thousands. Now they come in tens of thousands.

Objective observers like to claim that the gatherings have no relation to Jewish religious feeling. Young people come to the synagogue as they would to a club, in order to make new friends and learn new songs and dances. If they had someplace else to go, they wouldn't come to the synagogue.

I would say this explanation is not entirely correct. There is no lack of meeting places in Moscow; young people can get together either downtown, at the university or at the Komsomol* clubs. If they come to the synagogue, it is because they want to be among Jews and to be at one in their rejoicing with their fellow Jews all over the world, in spite of everything, and precisely because they have received an education of a different sort entirely. They come precisely because of the attempts that have been made to isolate them from their heritage, and they come in defiance of all efforts to make Judaism an object worthy of their hatred.

If they were allowed to live as Jews in a different way, in a different time, or in a different place, it is true that they would probably not gather together at the synagogue on this holiday of light and joy. But they have

---

* Soviet youth movement, attached to the Communist Party. T.N.

no alternative, and if they seize the excuse to come to Arkhipova Street, it is a sign that they wish to live as Jews . . . at least once a year, for one full evening. Somehow that will make them capable of waiting until the next time.

But it must not rain. . . .

I, too, had made preparations for the night of Simchat Torah,* as if for a great test or some meeting with the unknown. I was tense and restless. The many stories I had heard about the celebrations last year and the year before only increased my apprehension. I feared a disappointment. What if they didn't come? Or came, but not in great numbers? Or in great numbers, but not as Jews?

In order not to miss this meeting of three generations, I had arranged to spend the last days of Sukkot in Moscow. Unjustly, I had determined to rely neither on miracles nor on the Soviet airlines. I was afraid my plane might be delayed in Kiev or Leningrad, and I didn't want to arrive in Moscow at the last minute. I could not allow myself to miss this opportunity.

I might have seen the same thing in Leningrad . . . or so I was told. Thousands of students gather at the Leningrad synagogue on

* "Rejoicing of the Law"; last day of Sukkot festival, celebrating the completion of weekly Pentateuch readings in the synagogue and the beginning of a new cycle. T.N.

the night of Simchat Torah. In Tbilisi, too, young people crowd the synagogue even on an ordinary Sabbath. In Kiev I tried to convince myself that precisely because the Jewish leaders were attempting to suppress Jewish feeling and to drive away the younger generation, it would be worth staying to see what happened. But I was drawn to Moscow. Moscow would be the center; there the climax would occur. What would take place in Moscow could not happen anywhere else, inside Russia or abroad; so I had heard from people who had been there the past three years.

I wanted to see young people, to measure the extent of their Jewishness and discover its means of expression. I rehearsed dozens of questions to ask them, scarcely realizing that when the moment came I would forget them all. While traveling through Russia I had spoken mostly with the elderly or middle-aged. Many of them had expressed anxiety about the younger generation, its increasing estrangement and assimilation. They told me there was little hope for the perpetuation of Judaism in Russia. In America and Europe I had heard Russian representatives, Jewish and non-Jewish, who had taken the line of cold logic—there is no Jewish life in Russia simply because Jewish youth is not interested in it. It is for this reason alone that there are no

Yeshivot,* no Jewish grade schools, no Jewish clubs, no writers and no readers and no future. Judaism is strictly for the old. This explanation is put forth by everyone who comes from Moscow to speak about the "Jewish problem" in Russia. Full blame is placed upon the younger generation.

But tonight we would discover the truth. Youth itself would take the witness stand. It was years since I had last prepared for the night of Simchat Torah with such anticipation, such a sense of awe and excitement. I knew something would happen, something vast, a revelation. I was taut and fragile as the string on a violin. One must not force things, my friends cautioned me; you expect too much, you will never be satisfied with anything less than perfection. Patience. As the sun began to set, its rays danced in a fantasy of color over the Kremlin's gilded domes. The sky was clear and blue, and there were no clouds. The weather must hold. It must not rain.

It didn't. And it did not snow. There was a cold wind that cut to the bone. That's nothing, my friends said. Young people do not fear the cold. They'll come, if only to warm up.

Apparently the Soviet authorities also expected a large crowd, and they did their best

* Singular, Yeshivah: Rabbinic academy, institute for the training of rabbis. T.N.

to frighten it away. It had been made known that during the High Holy Days everyone entering the synagogue had been photographed. And now in front of the synagogue two gigantic floodlights had been installed, illuminating the entire street. The Jews were not to forget that someone was watching. The Jews would do well not to become too excited or to betray an overly Jewish character in their rejoicing.

They came nevertheless. Inside, the great hall of the synagogue was crammed with more than two thousand men and women. Many brought their children, for children, too, were to see that the Jews knew how to rejoice. The atmosphere was festive. Young girls stood among the men on the ground floor. The balcony was overflowing. People smiled at one another. Wherefore was this night different from all other nights? On all other nights we live in fear; tonight we are free men. Tonight one is permitted even to smile at strangers.

The old rabbi seemed calmer than he had on Yom Kippur. The hall buzzed with conversation. Eyes reflected hope and well-being. "Would you give your flag to my grandson?" an elderly man asked an Israeli child who held a pennant in his hand. The boy smiled and nodded. "Here you are." The Russian child took the Jewish flag and kissed it. An informer came up and demanded that the old man return the gift. He hesitated a second, took courage, then said no. His friends stood at his side. The informer bowed his head. Tonight he was alone.

When would the processions begin? They had long since finished the evening prayers. Why were they waiting? It seemed that they were just waiting; they had no special reason. They waited because it was pleasant to wait, because it was good to be in the midst of such a large and living crowd, in such a joyful place. If they didn't begin, they wouldn't have to end; they could treasure the perfection of the holiday. Expectation itself became part of the event. They drew it out, trying to expand the holiday past the limits of a single evening or a single day. If one could only remain here, united, until next year.

"Festivities are already under way outside," we were told by new arrivals.

The *gabbai* decided they had to begin. It was already late. One could not stay here all night, or even if one could, it would be dangerous. There was no knowing what people might do or say once they had been given a chance to release their feelings. There was no knowing what the repercussions would be from above.

They had to start. The *gabbai* banged on the table and shouted for silence. Useless. Thousands of whispers grew into an overwhelming roar. The *gabbai* continued shouting, but only those standing nearby, as we were, could hear him. The congregation had come to hear cries of a different sort, or perhaps not to hear anything, just to be present, to partake of the sacred joy of the holiday.

They began. Rabbi Yehuda-Leib Levin was honored with the first verse, "Thou has caused us to know . . ." He seemed to have recovered his youthful energy. His deep, sorrowful voice seemed more melodious. How many Jews in that hall fully understood his meaning when he sang, "For God is the Lord, there is no other beside Him"?

"The celebrating outside is incredible," we were told.

Inside, too, it was the same. The Israeli ambassador, Mr. Katriel Katz, was given the honor of reciting a verse, "Thy priests shall be clothed in righteousness, and thy faithful ones rejoice." His voice, too, was lost in the roar of whispers, but his title was known, and the enthusiasm mounted. People stood on tiptoe to see the representative of the sovereign state of Israel. His presence made them straighten up; they seemed taller.

The scrolls of the Torah were taken from the Ark and the dignitaries of the community invited to lead the first procession. The night before, I had participated in this ceremony in a small chamber where the *hasidim* pray. All the guests had been called for the first procession. Rabbi Levin had also been there, and we danced and danced until our strength gave out. We sang *hasidic* and Israeli songs in Yiddish and Hebrew. A tall, awkward, red-faced Jew had suddenly broken into the circle and caught the rabbi's arm. "Come, Rabbi, let us fulfill the commandment to dance! We must gladden our hearts for the Torah!" The two of them danced as we clapped our hands in time. The rabbi grew tired, but his partner goaded him on, more, more! They danced not for themselves but for the entire house of Israel. The tall one's happiness was mingled with rage. He could not sing, and he danced without rhythm in little jumps. His eyes shone with unworldly wrath, and I knew that his joy was real, flowing as it did out of an anger long contained. All year one is forbidden to be angry and forbidden to rejoice. Tonight one is permitted to rejoice. He was crying, too. Why, I do not know. Why does a man cry? Because things are good; because things are bad. Here the question is different; why does a man rejoice? Where does he get the strength to rejoice?

But that was last night, and they were *hasidim*. The people crowding into the synagogue tonight were simple Jews who had come to learn that it was possible to be a Jew and to find reasons for rejoicing . . . or to rejoice for no reason at all. Longbeards and workers, old and young, widows and lovely girls, students and bureaucrats. Among them there were many who had never prayed but who had come to watch the processions and to honor the Torah.

Processions? How could they lead a procession through this mob? The Jews formed an impenetrable living mass. No matter. Here everything was possible. It would take time, but no matter. They had the time, and patience too. Somehow the parade would pass. In the meantime they sang, louder and louder. They were all looking at us, the guests, as if to say, "Well, what's with you? Let's hear something from you." The entire Israeli diplomatic corps was present, together with their wives and children. We sang, "Gather our scattered ones from among the nations, and our dispersed from the corners of the world." Five times, ten times. A number of the diplomats belonged to left-wing parties. In their youth they had scorned religion, and religious people in particular. Tonight they celebrated the holiday with *hasidic* enthusiasm and abandon. Differences of opinion and class were left behind. An American writer once told me, "As I stood among the Jews of Russia, I became a Jew." He was not alone; many who come here as Israelis also return home as Jews.

"Outside they are turning the world upside down."

Should we go out? There was still time. Here, too, the world was in uproar. Men who had not sung for a year were raising their voices in song. Men who had not seen a Torah all year long were embracing and kissing it with a love bequeathed to them from generations past. Old men lifted their grandchildren onto their shoulders, saying, "Look, and remember." The children looked in wonder and laughed, uncertain what was happening. No matter; they would understand later, and they would remember. Tzvikah, the vocalist in the Israeli corps, assembled his chorus and gave them the pitch, "David, King of Israel, lives and endures." There was not a Jew in the hall who was not prepared to give his life defending that assertion.

The dignitaries had made their way back to the pulpit. The first procession was over. The *gabbai* announced that all guests were to take part in the second, and the congregation responded with new bursts of song. From one corner came an Israeli tune, "*Heivenu Shalom Aleichem*, We have brought peace unto you"; from another, "*Hava Nagilah*, Come let us rejoice." A third group preferred a traditional song, "Blessed is our God who created us in His honor and separated us from the nations and implanted in us eternal life." Instead of resisting one another, the various songs seemed to fuse into a single melodic affirmation. Those who had spent years in prison or in Siberia, those who had only recently become aware of their Jewishness, now proclaimed their unity: one people, one Torah. Each of them had stood once at the foot of Mount Sinai and heard the word, "*Anochi*—I am the Lord thy God." Each of them had received the promise of eternity.

We held the scrolls tightly to our chests and tried to make our way through the congregation. But instead of opening a path for us they pressed in closer, as if to block the way completely. They wanted us to stay among them. We were surrounded by a sea of faces, creased, joyful, unmasked. Hats of all kinds, skullcaps of every color, handkerchiefs in place of head covering. A young girl clapped her hands, an old man lifted up his eyes as if in prayer, a laborer sighed joyfully. Old men and their children and their children's children—everyone wanted to touch the Torah, to touch us. Everyone had something to whisper in our ears, a blessing or a secret. I have never in my life received so many blessings, never in my life been surrounded by so much good will and love. One pressed my hand, a second patted my arm, a third held my clothing. They would not let us move forward. They seemed to be trying to stop the progress of time. Through us they became freer, came closer to the reality of their dreams. They looked upon us as redeeming and protective angels. The fact that we were different, unafraid, was sufficient to elevate us in their eyes to the stature of saints and wonder workers. When I was young, we used to surround the holy *rebbe* in this fashion, begging him to intercede for us before the heavenly tribunal. But here, they asked for nothing. On the contrary, they brought us their gifts, their love, their blessings. Hundreds of them. Be healthy! Be strong! Be courageous! May we see you in the years to come! May we all live until that day! May you prosper! And may you sing! Do you hear? Just sing! A few went further, giving vent to their inmost feelings, but always in a whisper: I have a brother in Israel, a sister in Jerusalem, an uncle in Haifa. Short notices: brother, sister, grandfather, uncle, grandson. No names. They simply wanted us to know that a part of them was there, in the land of Israel. Others used clichés that in any other context would have produced smiles of condescension or contempt. "The people of Israel lives"; "the eternity of Israel shall not prove false"; "The redeemer shall come to Zion soon in our days." A Jew with a laborer's cap falling over his brow pushed forward and announced that he had something to tell me but no one was to hear.

He began to hum in my ear the words of *Hatikvah,** finished the first stanza, and disappeared, his face alight with victory. A woman pleaded with me, "Say something to my daughter. I brought her so she would see Jews who are not ashamed or afraid." The girl was very beautiful, dark and mysterious, with flashing eyes. She said something in Russian; I answered in Hebrew. Neither of us understood the other; yet somehow we did. Her mother was satisfied; she kissed my hand, murmuring, "Thank you, thank you. Will we ever see you again?" I didn't know what to say. I forgot everything I knew, except those two words: Thank you, thank you. Thank you for the gift of this moment, thank you for being alive, for enduring, for knowing how to rejoice and to hope and to dream. Thank you for being Jews like us. And a thousand and one thanks for finding the strength to thank a Jew like me for being a Jew.

Our procession lasted about an hour. Pale and drenched with sweat, we relinquished the Torah scrolls to the next group of marchers and returned to our seats in the visitors' section. I was out of breath and exhausted. I wanted to rest, close my eyes and wait for my strength to return. The third procession had begun. The singing reached me as if from a

---

*Israel national anthem (The Hope). T.N.

great distance or from behind a curtain, as in a daydream. I had never imagined that the weight and power of this experience would stun me as it did. If I had come for this alone, it would have been sufficient.

"They're going crazy out there. We must join them."

We went. The remaining processions we would celebrate outside. Luckily there was a side door; we did not have to pass through the congregation. They would never have let us go. Two or three "agents" got up to follow us. Let them. The Prince of the Torah protects those who come to rejoice in His name.

The street was unrecognizable. For a second I thought I had been transported to another world, somewhere in Israel or in Brooklyn. Angels and seraphim were serenading the night; King David played his harp. The city burst with gladness and joy. The evening had just begun.

6

A Night of Dancing

Deliberately or not, they had been lying to us. With good intentions or bad, they had misinformed us. They wanted us to despair of Jewish youth in Russia, had attempted to persuade us of its increasing alienation from Jewish life. For years they had spread such lies, supporting them with arguments whose logic was hard to refute. After all, we were talking about the third generation after the Revolution. Even if they wished to be Jewish, where would they begin? Even if they wanted to study Torah, who was there to help them? It is only natural that they have forgotten their past; tomorrow they will have nothing to forget. And we listened, were saddened, but concurred. Yes, there was something to that. What can one do? It was the inevitable result of historical materialism. You cannot demand the impossible.

But they surprised us. Soviet Jewish youth has remained Jewish to a degree beyond anything we could possibly have expected.

I do not know where all these young people came from. They didn't tell me, although I asked. Perhaps there is no one answer, but tens of thousands that are all the same. No matter —they came.

Who sent them? Who persuaded them to come running to spend a Jewish holiday in a Jewish atmosphere and in accordance with traditional Jewish custom? Who told them when and where and why? I was unable to discover. Perhaps they knew but preferred not to say in public. Fine. Let them preserve their secret. All that matters is that they have one and that they came.

Still, there is something strange about it. Tens of thousands of youngsters do not suddenly emerge from nowhere at a specified time and place. Someone had to organize and direct them; someone had to make the contacts, maintain the necessary spirit, and inform them of the date and time. Who made all the preparations? Who breathed the spark into a flame? I didn't ask; they wouldn't have answered. Perhaps it is better for me not to know.

They came in droves. From near and far, from downtown and the suburbs, from the university and from the factories, from school dormitories and from the Komsomol club. They came in groups; they came alone. But once here, they became a single body, voicing a song of praise to the Jewish people and its will to live.

How many were there? Ten thousand? Twenty thousand? More. About thirty thousand. The crush was worse than it had been inside the synagogue. They filled the whole street, spilled over into courtyards, dancing and singing, dancing and singing. They seemed to hover in midair, Chagall-like, floating above the mass of shadows and colors below, above time, climbing a Jacob's ladder that reached to the heavens, if not higher.

Tomorrow they would descend and scatter, disappear into the innermost parts of Moscow, not to be heard from for another year. But they would return and bring more with them. The line will never break; one who has come will always return.

I moved among them like a sleepwalker, stunned by what I saw and heard, half disbelieving my own senses. I had known they would come, but not in such numbers; I had known they would celebrate, but not that their celebration would be so genuine and so deeply Jewish.

They sang and danced, talked among themselves or with strangers. They were borne along on a crest that seemed incapable of breaking. Their faces reflected a special radiance, their eyes the age-old flame that burned in the house of their ancestors—to which they seemed finally to have returned.

I was swept along in the current, passing from one group to another, from one circle to the next, sharing their happiness and absorbing the sound of their voices.

It was after ten. The cold brought tears to one's eyes. But it was easy to warm up; one had only to join in the singing or start talking with someone.

A girl strummed her guitar and sang a Yiddish folk song, "Buy my cigarettes, take pity on a poor orphan." A few steps away, a boy played *Heivenu Shalom Aleichem* on the accordion. Further on, others were dancing the *hora*. Still another group was heatedly debating Judaism and Israel. "I am a communist!" a young student shouted. I asked him what he was doing here. "I am also a Jew." Suddenly I wanted to go from one to the other, begging their forgiveness for our lack of faith. Our disappointment in Russian Jewish youth is a thing of our own creating. It is they who reassure us, they who teach us not to despair.

Hour after hour I wandered through that

street, which had become a rallying point for pilgrims from every corner of the city. It seemed to have lengthened and widened, become a thing of joy and beauty. It seemed to have taken on a new soul and with it the sanctity of a heavenly dream.

A dark-haired and vivacious girl stood in the middle of a circle, leading a chorus of voices in a series of questions and answers.

"Who are we?"

"Jews!"

"What are we?"

"jews!"

"What shall we remain?"

"Jews!"

They laughed as they chanted their responses. Someone translated the dialogue for me, urged me to join in the laughter and handclapping. It was a splendid joke. The Kremlin was ten minutes away, and the echoes of the Jewish celebration reached to the tomb of Stalin. "It's too crowded here!" a boy cried. "Next year we celebrate in Red Square!" His audience burst into applause.

"Who are we?" asked the dark-haired girl.

"Jews!"

A little later I went up to talk with her. Would she speak to a stranger? She would. Not afraid? No, not tonight. And other nights? Let's stick to tonight. She was a hu-

manities major at the university. She spoke
Yiddish, she said, with her grandfather, sometimes with her parents, and occasionally even
with friends when they were alone. Was she
religious? Far from it; never had been. Her
parents had been born after the Revolution,
and even they had received an antireligious
education. What did she know about the
Jewish religion? That it was based on outdated
values. And about the Jewish people? That
it was made up of capitalists and swindlers.
And the state of Israel? That it was aggressive,
racist, and imperialist. Where had she learned
all this? From textbooks, government pam-
phlets, and the press. I asked her why she
insisted on remaining Jewish. She hesitated,
searching for the proper word, then smiled.
"What does it matter what they think of us
. . . it's what we think that counts." And she
added immediately, "I'll tell you why I'm a
Jew. Because I like to sing."

The songs they sang were mostly products
of the nineteenth century. The most popular
was a Yiddish folk song, "Come let us go together, all of us together, and greet the bride
and groom." But they had updated the lyrics,
substituting for the last phrase, "Come let us
greet the Jewish people," or "the people of
Israel," or "the God of Israel and His Torah."
One group of students had formed a human

pyramid. The young man at the apex was yelling defiantly, "Nothing can help them! We shall overcome them!" His audience roared back, "Hurrah! Hurrah!"

More cheers came from a nearby group that was celebrating the holiday in a manner decidedly Russian, tossing one of their number into the air. Five times, six, seven. Higher, higher. A girl pleaded with them to stop, but they paid no attention. Eight times, nine, ten. Nothing would happen. Nothing did. A carpet of outstretched hands was waiting to catch the hero upon his return from on high. "Hurrah! Hurrah!"

This is how Russian soldiers celebrated their victory over the Germans, and how the Jews celebrate their triumph over despair.

"What does anyone in America or Israel care if my passport is stamped 'Jewish'? It doesn't matter to me, and it doesn't matter to these young people here tonight. So stop protesting about things that don't bother us. We have long since ceased being ashamed of our Jewishness. We can't hide it anyway. Besides, by accepting it we've managed to turn obedience to the law into an act of free choice."

The man I was talking to had served as a captain in the Red Army and had been decorated in Berlin. Like his father before him, he was a sworn communist. But like all the rest, he suffered on account of his Jewishness. Were he Russian he would have long ago been appointed a full professor at the university. He was still holding an instructorship in foreign languages. One day, he said, he decided that as long as they made him feel like a Jew, he might as well act accordingly. It was the only way to beat them at their own game. "Two years ago I came to the synagogue on the night of Simchat Torah. I wanted to see Jews, and I wanted to be with them. I didn't tell my wife, who isn't Jewish, or my sixteen-year-old son. Why should I burden him with problems? There was time enough for that. I came back last year for the second time. The youngsters were singing and dancing, almost like tonight. I found myself suddenly in the middle of a group of youngsters, and my heart stopped.... I was standing face to face with my son. He said he'd been coming for the past three years, but hadn't dared to tell me.

"Would you like to see him?" he asked me.

"Yes, very much."

"He's here, somewhere," he said, gesturing at the crowd as if to say, "Look closely, they are all my son."

I talked with dozens of people. Some of them questioned me incessantly about the Jews abroad; others tried to debate with me the issue of diplomatic relations between Israel and

Germany; a few almost openly acknowledged that they suffered because they were Jews. But not one of them criticized the state or the Russian authorities. And they all claimed, "They will never succeed. Jewish youth in Russia will not disappoint us."

Anyone who was there that night can attest to the truth of this statement. Young Jews in Russia want to return to Judaism, but without knowing what it is. Without knowing why, they define themselves as Jews. And they believe in the eternity of the Jewish people, without the slightest notion of the meaning of its mission. That is their tragedy.

Ilya Ehrenburg wrote in his memoirs that he would call himself a Jew as long as a single anti-Semite remained on earth. There is no doubt that this way of thinking is an important factor in bringing young people together at the synagogue to rejoice in the Torah. Precisely because it is not easy to be a Jew in Russia, Jewish consciousness will continue to grow. "We are Jews for spite," one student said to me. There is some accuracy in this. For want of better teachers, it is the anti-Semites who are making them Jews.

I said to one of them, "You don't know Hebrew, you never learned Jewish history, you don't fulfill the commandments, and you don't believe in the God of Israel—in what way are you a Jew?"

He answered, "Apparently you live in a country where Jews can afford the luxury of asking questions. Things are different here. It's enough for a Jew to call himself a Jew. It's enough to fulfill one commandment or to celebrate one Jewish day a year. With us, being Jewish is not a matter of words, but of simple endurance, not of definition but of existence. If my son were to ask me one day what a Jew is, I would tell him that a Jew is one who knows when to ask questions and when to give answers . . . and when to do neither."

"Hurrah!" the voices thundered. "David, King of Israel, lives and endures. Hurrah!"

This evening gave me new hope and encouragement. We need not despair. The Jews in Kiev, Leningrad, and Tbilisi who had complained to me about the doubtful future of Russian Jewry were wrong. They were too pessimistic, and apparently did not know their own children or the hidden forces which prompt them, at least once a year, to affirm their sense of community. Everyone has judged this generation guilty of denying its God and of being ashamed of its Jewishness. They are said to despise all mention of Israel. But it is a lie. Their love for Israel exceeds that of young Jews anywhere else in the world.

If, on this night of dancing, gladness finally

overcame fear, it was because of them. If song triumphed over silence, it was their triumph. And it was through them only that the dream of freedom and community became reality. I am still waiting to see tens of thousands of Jews singing and dancing in Times Square or the Place de l'Etoile as they danced here, in the heart of Moscow, on the night of Simchat Torah. They danced until midnight without rest, to let the city know that they are Jews.

7

Solitude

The Jew who came up to me in a dark side
street in Leningrad seemed older and wiser
than his years. But perhaps he was not wise
at all, only naïve; or perhaps the experience
of despair had led him to develop an acute
sense of irony; or, who knows, perhaps he
was wholly insane.

"We prayed together in the synagogue this
morning," he said, as if to justify himself. "I
was waiting for a chance to talk to you alone."

Five hours had passed since morning
prayers. I had not noticed him, although since
then he had trailed me to the library, to my
hotel, and through a museum exhibit. He
hadn't dared come nearer until he was sure
that we weren't being followed.

"I am at your service. We can talk now, if you like."

He was wearing a winter coat and was breathing heavily. The walk had tired him. A smile lay frozen on his thin face. His movements were slow. All the world's undefined weariness seemed to have settled in his large eyes.

"I have a number of questions. I would be grateful if you would be kind enough to answer them."

He has a brother in Israel, I thought, or in America, and he wants me to locate him. Dozens of Jews had approached me with similar requests. It is hard to find a Jewish family in Russia that has not been torn from its relatives. Everyone who comes from abroad turns into a Bureau of Missing Persons. Do you know Leib Finkelstein in Philadelphia? Sam Rosenberg in New Jersey? Isaac Stein in Petah Tikvah? You always say yes. Or that you know someone who knows them. You promise to get in touch.

"You don't understand. I just want to ask questions. I don't need help . . . only information."

I looked at him again. Maybe he really was unbalanced? I waited for an explanation, but instead he began a strange monologue, answering his own questions, explaining away his own doubts. He didn't give me a chance to say a word, but held me there as a witness to his thoughts. I was simply to listen and to remember.

"They say there are three million Jews in New York, hah? I don't believe it. And that in all of America the number comes to six million, hah? I don't believe it. I hear there are statesmen and rich industrialists, rabbis and writers and community workers, and that they're all devoted to their people, dedicated to their work? I just don't believe it. If it were true, we would *know* about it. Don't come to me with fairy tales. The truth is, there are no Jews in America or anywhere else. Only here."

If he had been in a rage, I would have been less moved by what he said. But his speech was quiet and restrained, devoid of any bitterness or complaint. It occurred to me suddenly that I was right the first time. The man did have a brother in America, more than one. In his own way he was trying to locate six million lost brothers and exchange with them a sign of life. It was the only way to overcome his solitude.

In Kiev, on the second day of Sukkot, I left the synagogue after morning prayers and started toward the Hotel Dnieper, where I had a room. I sensed that I was being followed. Turning around suddenly, I saw three Jews standing some distance from me. They had stopped when I had. I felt sorry for them; they must have been sent by the *gabbai* to keep an eye on me. I shrugged my shoulders and continued walking. They followed.

A few minutes later I heard one of them quicken his pace. I slowed down and waited for him to overtake me. "I have to talk to you," he hissed at me in Yiddish. "It's too dangerous inside. One must beware of informers." I expected him to tell me next that his two friends worked as agents. Similarly grotesque incidents had befallen me in Leningrad and Moscow. I smiled at him, "Aren't you afraid?"

"I've taken precautions. My friends will stay back there to warn me."

He began to describe in gloomy terms the condition of the 150,000 Jews in Kiev. Nothing new. It was all very general, almost routine by now. The same thing goes on in Minsk and Vilna, in Cracow and Odessa. Only here, there is a long tradition of anti-Semitism, from Chmielnitzki to Babi Yar, providing an added element in the general pattern of terror. The conciliatory enactments of the municipal government have not succeeded in allaying Jewish fears. Legislation and reality are two different and often opposing things. Of the three hundred synagogues and *shtiblach* (prayer rooms) Kiev once had, only one remains open.

He broke off almost in the middle of a sentence and returned to his companions, sending one of them to continue the account. In twenty minutes the third took his turn. Each of them knew what the one before had said; there was no repetition. One spoke about the chief *gabbai* and his cruelty toward the old rabbi; another told about Jews who were still in prison on charges of Zionist-nationalist activity or on suspicion of having committed "economic crimes"; the third stressed the impending doom of Russian Jewry—only a miracle could help.

All three asked the same questions. Why are the Jews outside so silent? Why aren't they doing something? Don't they know what is happening here? Or don't they want to know? Maybe it's easier not to know, to ignore our suffering and carry on with their daily affairs, to act as if we didn't exist.

I could not answer their questions. Why *is* the Jewish world so indifferent to the Jews in Russia? I don't know. I know only that this apathy, from an historical point of view, borders on the criminal. Even if we assume that our protests are useless to change Kremlin policy, they do change the spiritual climate for the Jewish population. They bring Soviet Jews the comforting knowledge of a single fact—that the Jewish people have not forgotten them, that they are not alone.

Justly or unjustly, they think we have forgotten; they think that we have ignored or abandoned them, that somehow we are all too busy and preoccupied to be interested in their fate. Jewish solidarity extends to everyone in the world but them. The Jewish state has even begun to help the nations of Asia and Africa, but toward them it displays an attitude of vague and hesitant indifference.

This, more than anything else, is what pains them. They can overcome the rest. After all, they are a people who have never been strangers to persecution and discrimination. They will endure, despite the fear which permeates their collective existence. They will submit to neither the pressures nor the seductions of their environment. I repeat that I am not as pessimistic as they are; the youngsters I saw dancing on Simchat Torah convinced me that the end is not yet in sight, the fountain has not yet run dry. But how are they to overcome the pain that springs from within, their disappointment in us and the desperate conclusions they are inevitably forced to draw about us?

We must realize that the Russian government wants them to feel cut off from world Jewry. The official press censors every news item concerning Jewish action taken on their behalf. It failed to report the march in Washington or the demonstration at Madison Square

Garden. The government's purpose is clear: to convince the Russian Jews to abandon their illusory expectations of help from America or Western Europe. They are to depend solely on the good will of the Kremlin, and would, therefore, do well to know their place and to behave accordingly. They may as well forget about the Jewish people abroad, who have betrayed them, or who at the very least regard them as stepchildren.

They do of course receive some news from other sources. They listen to foreign shortwave broadcasts in Russian and Yiddish. The BBC, the Voice of America, and the Voice of Israel provide them with information missing from their local papers. But it is not enough; it is a drop in the ocean. A man needs a strong will to withstand brainwashing.

A number of times I was asked by Russian Jews to detail the various efforts being undertaken abroad in their behalf. I confess that I was ashamed to reveal the truth. I could not bring myself to tell them that only a few thousand Jews went to Washington to take part in the protest march; that the Jews of New York were apparently too busy to fill Madison Square Garden for the demonstration held early in 1965 for the Jews of Russia. I lied to them, exaggerating the figures, told them that a hundred thousand Jews had assembled on that evening. They looked at me in simple amazement. What? Only a hundred thousand? A hundred thousand out of three million? Is that all?

"Our sense of isolation is a compound of several elements," a professor in a large city told me. "From the Russian point of view we are considered second-class citizens, living on the fringes of society. The new regime has made life easier for everyone but us, or, to be perfectly objective, not in the same way for us. The freedoms it granted to others reached us in truncated form. Nevertheless, this is a form of isolation we can live with. It is the isolation that derives from your relations with us that is so difficult to understand. We feel that we have been expelled by the Jewish people, that we are condemned to live on the borders of Jewish history, that we are not worth the effort of protest. Where we are concerned, there is no point in making sacrifices or in trying to bring about change. You have despaired of us, and you behave as if we didn't exist, as if we were not a part of the Jewish people. See for yourself. The Iron Curtain is gradually being raised . . . it is even beginning to disappear . . . but at the very same time the curtain of solitude is falling more heavily all around us."

A religious Jew told me, "Once upon a time Jews used to declare a day of prayer or a day of fasting to protest the maltreatment of a

Jewish community, whether near or far. Tell me, how many such days have you held, and where?"

This is the most powerfully affecting aspect of their plight. I do not like to draw extreme parallels between the condition of the Jews in Russia and that of the European Jews during the Holocaust. The analogy is illogical, unfair, and unreal. But from a subjective and emotional point of view it is impossible to escape the impression that the two communities have something in common: a sense of total isolation.

And for this state of affairs it is we, not the Soviet authorities, who will one day be called to judgment. We as well as they are guilty. If we are unable to force Moscow to accept Russian Jews as citizens with equal rights, we can at least make contact with them, so that they may know that their welfare concerns us, that they, too, are our brothers.

Their isolation is so total and absolute that they will do anything to break out, even for a minute. If they fall upon you, begging for a prayer book, a Jewish calendar, a *talith*,* it is not simply because they are religious; they want something to link them to the rest of their people, something to remind them that

* Ritual prayer shawl. T.N.

somewhere Jewish history continues to be written. Frequently I was approached by young people who wanted anything I could give them, anything at all, so long as it was Jewish. One took the Hebrew newspaper I had in my hand and folded it away in his pocket. For a souvenir, he said, to remind him of the Jews and in the hope that they would remind themselves of him.

The Jews who throng the synagogues do not all come to pray. They come to see Jews, to be in Jewish company, and, if luck is with them, to be near a Jew from abroad. Somewhere in their souls they harbor a dream of unity. Hour after hour they remain in the synagogue. Nowhere else in the world have I seen prayers last so long. On a holiday or even a Sabbath the morning service goes on until one or two in the afternoon. The cantor sings slowly, drawing out every line, every note. No one becomes restless. The congregation loves it; the later they go home, the better. In the meantime they spend another hour together, and another, on the one island of comfort they have preserved in a sea of solitude.

The true source of their comfort, however, lies elsewhere, in the knowledge that there are other Jews in the world, whether near or far, who live in freedom, faithful Jews who are not haunted by shadows of fear but proudly evidence their Jewishness for all to see. They crowd around a visitor, questioning him closely about the Jewish communities in America, Western Europe, and, of course, Israel. Young and old, religious or communist, student or bureaucrat, they prefer to ask rather than answer. Rather than hear your assurances that things will improve for them as well, they want to know whether things will be good or are already good for you, for all those who have been privileged to settle in countries where the word Jew is not a mark of shame. They refuse to talk about themselves; only rarely can you elicit more than a low sigh. They have nothing heretical to say about the regime, and will not criticize government policy. They prefer to listen.

When you tell them that Israel is not on the brink of destruction, that world Jewry is not disintegrating, that Jewish youth in the Diaspora actively identifies with its people, they look satisfied and content. Through you they become aware of themselves as part of a large and vital body. When you tell them that Jews who hold high office in the United States still remain Jews in word and deed, you have justified their faith and made them glad. When they hear of Jewish authors in France who have gained world reputations, of men in Israel who have become legendary figures all over the globe, of American scientists who continue to fulfill the commandments of Judaism, their faces light up with joy and pride.

They have harsh claims to make against world Jewry, but still they pray for its welfare and security. More than once, in Moscow and elsewhere, I was told, "The thought that you are continuing to build a Jewish future in Israel and the West is what helps us to endure. Without that, without you, who knows if we could keep going. . . ."

How much they need to believe in us came home to me in a small and secluded synagogue I had gone to visit during Sukkot. There were about eight hundred Jews there, and I was given the honor of reciting the Haphtarah.* They looked at me in silence as I chanted the words of the prophets, but their faces were wet with tears. Why did they weep? It was not in sadness or despair. They wept because they had been made to see that there are still young Jews in the world who can read from the Torah, who have not forgotten the melodies of prayer, who turn to their tradition still as to a fountain of living waters.

Without our knowing it and perhaps without our willing it, we have become their support. Their love for us forges their will to live, although we are always too busy to reply in kind.

* Prophetic lesson read on Sabbaths after weekly portion of Pentateuch. T.N.

The Jew I met on a side street in Leningrad told me that today the only real Jews live in Russia. Nowhere else. To our eternal shame, he may be right.

8

The Dream
of Israel

If there is one place in the world where the state of Israel is regarded not as a territorial unit operating according to its own laws and within its own borders, but as a distant dream filling the veins of reality with sacred blood, that place is the Soviet Union. It is only the Jews of Russia who have yet to be infected with cynicism toward the Jewish state, who still identify the earthly Jerusalem with its heavenly counterpart, the eternal city that embraces a Temple of Fire.

Isolated behind walls of fear and silence, the Jews of Russia know nothing of the secular affairs of Israel, nothing of the scandals, of the petty political squabbles. They would not believe it anyway. For them the Jewish state is wrapped in a prayer shawl of purest blue. Its citizens are all righteous men and heroes; otherwise, they would not be living there.

It happened on Yom Kippur in the Great Synagogue of Moscow. Outside it was already dark. The last prayer was almost over. Old men wept as the gates of heaven began to close; the Book of Judgment was being sealed —who shall live and who shall die, who shall be set free and who shall be afflicted. Their tears were a last effort to rend the skies and avert some terrible decree.

The hall was tense and crowded; the worshipers perspired heavily, suffocating from the heat and the effects of their day-long fast. No one complained. Outside, a large crowd was trying to push its way in. There was no room, but somehow they would manage. If there were places for two thousand, there would be places for three. An air of expectancy swept over the congregation.

Something was about to happen. They seemed nervous, serious, as if preparing for a dire and momentous act, a collective act that would be remembered forever.

The cantor finished the last prayer for forgiveness. He quickened his pace, as if rushing toward some critical event. Our Father our King, seal us in the Book of Life. Our Father our King, do it for the sake of the little children. Everyone seemed to be standing on tiptoe. *Kaddish.* Another minute. They counted the seconds. The cantor proclaimed, "*Adonai hu haElohim*, God is the Lord!" Seven times, with the congregation responding after him. The old sexton brought the *shofar.** T'kiah!*** The congregation held its breath. And then it happened. As if in response to a mysterious command from an unknown source, three thousand Jews turned as one body toward the visitors' section, stood up straight and tall, facing the representatives of Israel, looking directly into their eyes, as if trying to read in them their past and their future, the secret of their existence. Then in the awful mounting silence they suddenly burst into a wild spontaneous cry which seemed to issue from a single throat, a single heart: "Next year in Jerusalem! Next year in Jerusalem! Next year in Jerusalem!"

The dramatic intensity of this moment immediately brought to my mind similar occurrences in the Middle Ages, when, with a single nod of the head, with a single declaration of faith, Jews sanctified the Name and died. No

* Memorial prayer. T.N.

** Ram's horn, blown during the High Holy Days as a call to repentance. T.N.

*** Designation for a prolonged blast on the *shofar*. T.N.

one had forced them; of their own free will they had repeated an ancient promise, "We shall do, and we shall listen." Instinctively, without preparation or prior instruction, they had slipped back hundreds of years. Their silence, like their cry, is to be understood not as a prayer, but as an oath of fidelity.

Some will say: double loyalties. But they will not understand that the loyalty of these Jews does not extend to a foreign power but to a concept and a vision, not to a foreign government but to longings which the act of fidelity itself both defines and symbolizes. For the Jews of Russia, Israel is not simply a geographical location but an abstract messianic principle, a part of their own inner spiritual life. It is perhaps strange that in the homeland of Marxist rationalism there are still Jews who think of Israel as some kind of miracle and speak of it in terms that sound to us like the tritest and most pious of clichés. These Jews have not yet learned to enclose the word Zionism in quotation marks.

There is of course no lack of professional faultfinders. Just read the official press, which portrays Israel as an atavistic, racist, aggressive, and colonialist state, its leaders thorough scoundrels and its citizens exploited and defenseless captives—a kingdom of hell on earth. In one of the larger Russian cities, a government guide told me that a few years ago the Israeli Air Force had attempted to blow up the pyramids . . . in order to ruin the Egyptian tourist industry! He had heard this from "reliable sources." He also knew that in front of the Knesset* building in Jerusalem there is a sign proclaiming that the state will not rest content until it has reconquered Mount Zion, which is situated, he averred, somewhere between Alexandria and Cairo. Similarly, he was prepared to swear on his life that Israel wants war, that it is allied with Nazi criminals in Germany, and that within its borders there is no such thing as individual liberty.

The purpose of such propaganda is to make Israel seem hateful not only to the general populace but to the Jews as well, to undermine the esteem in which they hold the Jewish state, and to convince them finally to relinquish an idea which has failed, a vision of redemption which has somehow been made profane. Jewish readers of Russian newspapers are invited to see for themselves that what takes place in the Jewish state is a violation rather than a fulfillment of their ancestors' millenial dream. Ruled by reactionaries, it is a state which persecutes minorities, oppresses the weak, and exploits the poor. How much better then for Russian Jews to turn their

*Parliament of Israel. T.N.

backs and blot all memory of Israel from their minds and their hearts.

This form of psychological warfare, directed less against the Jewish state than against the Jewish dream, has thus far failed to achieve its objective. It will continue to fail in the future. The Russian authorities do not understand that the Jews and they are speaking two different languages, are talking about two different things. They fail to understand that it is possible to malign the earthly Jerusalem without injuring in the slightest the Jerusalem which Jews treasure in their dreams as a city innocent of any stain or flaw; their fidelity to that Jerusalem is in essence fidelity to themselves. It is for this reason that they value anything that comes from Israel and honor anyone who comes in its name.

Jews in New York, Paris, or London, even in Tel Aviv, are far more critical of Israel than are most Russian Jews. Somehow, we have all become used to judging Israel by routine secular standards; the hope of yesterday has become today's fact. We have learned to draw clear and distinct lines between dream and reality. But in Russia, Jews have yet to reach this stage of maturity. The simple day-to-day words which produce no reaction in us whatsoever are often capable of reducing them to a state of extreme sentimental emotion. In Moscow I saw a Jew burst into tears when a little girl from Israel said something to him in Hebrew. I sometimes think that if Israel had been established solely for the sake of the Russian Jews, it would have fulfilled its purpose. If it existed solely to demonstrate to them that they must not despair, that a dream is indeed capable of becoming reality, that would have been sufficient.

On the other hand, it may be that our reality exists only, or at least partly, by virtue of their dream.

Were the gates suddenly to open, would all three million Jews in Russia decide to leave and go to Israel? I cannot answer that question. No one can. It is dangerous, and almost impossible to generalize on this subject.

I did on occasion meet Jews who exclaimed to me, "If only they would load us all on a great cart and send us off to Israel!" But I also talked with young people who said the opposite, "We are not prepared to become immigrants in a new land and begin our lives all over again."

Once, some years ago, during the Stalin era, word came down that Jews would be permitted to register for exit visas. Thousands responded, and they were all imprisoned. Ever since, the Jews have feared a repetition of this incident. Even many of those who have close relatives in Israel, brothers and sisters, hesitate to apply for emigration permits. They prefer to wait . . . and to be silent.

So it is impossible to determine in advance precisely what would happen if and when the hoped for miracle should occur. There are those who believe we will witness a mass movement that will surpass in numbers and enthusiasm all previous emigrations to the land of Israel. Fifty years of communist rule they argue, have proved to the Jews that no matter what they do, they will always remain an unwanted element in Russian society, denied the right to live as Jews and yet, as Jews, unable wholly to assimilate into non-Jewish society. Therefore, in the absence of any alternative, young and old alike will take the necessary final step and leave for a country that awaits them with open arms.

Others claim that only the aged will go and perhaps a small percentage of the young. Most young people will draw back at the last minute. They are not prepared to leave for all time the country in which they were born, brought up, and educated, whose language they love, and whose customs they know. The frequency of intermarriage among the young will prove to be another important deterrent. Despite the magical appeal of Israel and despite pressures at home, they will forego the opportunity to emigrate and will remain in Russia.

It is hard to determine which of these two readings is the more plausible. In deciding such questions, one could not rely on the findings of a public opinion poll or questionnaire, even if one dared to undertake such a survey. As in many other areas, we may speak with relative certainty only of subjective impressions.

During my travels I talked with older men, their children, and their grandchildren. I paid a number of visits to their homes and tried to sound them out. On the plane from Moscow to Leningrad I spoke with an electrical engineer; in Kiev I met a factory foreman; in Tbilisi I took a walk with a professor of political science; and in Moscow I spent many hours with students.

From everything they said and did not say, I came to the conclusion that many Russian Jews would seize an opportunity to flee the fear and discrimination which pursue them. To be more precise, the few would draw the many after them. Once it began, once permission was granted and the first gate opened, they would follow in multitudes. It has always been that way in Jewish history. Few have ever chosen to remain behind, alone.

But I should emphasize that if the Jews of Russia leave their homes it will not be because they oppose the regime or because the objective conditions of their lives are unbearable. Many Russian citizens share those same conditions. They will leave only because of the anti-Jewish atmosphere which—no matter who is at fault—pervades their homeland. Were they allowed to live full Jewish lives, were they not coerced into disowning their tradition, it is very likely that many of them would prefer to remain rather than set out for the unknown.

But as a Jew in Kiev said to me, "If only this theoretical question became a real one, then we could do without answers."

There is no doubt, however, that Israel occupies a vital and central place in the consciousness of Russian Jews at all ages and all levels. Jews are interested in news from Israel not simply out of curiosity but out of a profound sense of shared purpose. They feel that what happens there also affects them, that their fate is linked with that of the Jewish state. And if they still dream of a messianic future, it is because there, across the sea, an attempt has already been made to establish a third Temple, a third Jewish Commonwealth. From afar, in thought and silent prayer, they strive to take part in that endeavor.

In virtually every Jewish home everyone listens to the broadcasts of the Voice of Israel. In every city I received the latest news from

Israel at the synagogue. Members of the congregation would come up to me and whisper
the content of Premier Levi Eshkol's latest
speech in Tel Aviv, the words of Golda Meir
at an assembly of the United Nations, or the
most recent threats of Gamal Abdel Nasser.
They importune tourists to tell them more and
more about life in Israel. Somehow they still
find it hard to believe that a Jewish state exists,
with its own ministers and its own police
force, its own army and its own heroes. They
know it is all true, but it sounds like a dream.
Again and again they ask you if the state is
really all that strong, if its army is really capable of defeating the enemy, if its scientists
are really internationally known, if its presence
in Africa is really felt as much as that of the
United States or the Soviet Union.

When you tell them what they want to
hear, something takes fire in their eyes; they
regard you as a messenger from a land of
dreams, as the scion of a royal house. The
waves of love I felt on the night of Simchat
Torah in the Moscow synagogue were another expression of their reverence for the
Jewish state and its significance for them.
Their tears, their secret handshakes, their whispered messages and cautious touches, their
short blessings, all indicated that I was a different kind of Jew from them, a kind they
would like to become . . . unafraid, and free

to express their feelings about the state of Israel. I shall never forget the Jew who came up to me in the synagogue and almost without moving his lips said under his breath, "I spent ten years in a prison and a labor camp for so-called Jewish nationalist activities; now I know that it was worth it." Or the sociology student who suddenly began to talk to me in broken Hebrew, in phrases that seemed to be taken out of a beginners' textbook, "This is a house. This is a man. This is a window. I am a Jew." That was all he said before he disappeared with a smile into the crowd.

And how can I forget the young people singing in Hebrew? The girls teaching their boyfriends Yiddish and Israeli songs which they had learned God knows how and God knows where; or the melancholy look of the waitress who saw the Hebrew newspaper in my hand? The hundreds of Jews who in a thousand different ways and through multifarious means always succeeded in identifying themselves to me, with a wink of the eye, a Hebrew word—how can I forget them?

"If something should happen to Israel, we would be totally lost. If that hope also explodes, we will no longer be able to hold out, we will have to submit." This was the opinion of a technician, about forty years old, who was born in Russia, studied in a Russian high school and university, served in the Red Army, and was wounded twice in the service of his homeland.

"If you could emigrate to Israel," I asked him, "would you go?"

He was a communist. "That is a question I'd rather not think about."

A paradox, perhaps. Can one be loyal to two opposing ideas at the same time? Apparently so. For the Jews of Russia everything is possible. It must be, or they would have given up long ago.

A communist student tried to argue with me one evening about relations between Israel and Germany. He had prepared all the right questions. "Why have they sold weapons and uniforms to the Bundeswehr? Why did they approve German rearmament? Why have they established diplomatic ties with Bonn?"

To be truthful, I did not feel very comfortable with these questions. I have my own opinions on this subject. But Moscow was not the proper place in which to begin criticizing Israel's German policy. Instead, I answered with another question. "Is it all right for Moscow to do this? Is Moscow permitted to encourage trade relations with Bonn? Or to defend the legitimacy of East Germany? Why did Russia extend such a warm welcome to Alfred Krupp? • And why are there more Ger-

• German industrialist whose factories produced arms for the Third Reich during World War II. T.N.

man tourists in Russia than any other kind?"

"That's different," he said finally, in some confusion. "Don't compare Israel to Russia."

He did not understand what he was saying. He did not realize that he, too, applied a different standard to Israel, that his relation to the Jewish state was qualitatively different even from his relation to Russia. He expected Israel to be pure and holy; Israel must not soil her hands.

An ancient proverb says: God bestowed two gifts upon men. To some he gave the gift of wine, and to some the faculty of thirst.

He gave the reality of Israel to us; the dream of Israel he left to the Jews of Russia. We are in need of them, just as they are in need of us. Perhaps more.

9

What They Expect from Us

The holidays were over, and the Jewish spirit had once more gone underground. The three generations who had come together for prayer and song once more went their separate ways. Everyone went home, back to work, back to the university; the side streets with their little synagogues took on their usual abandoned look. Only those above forty would appear for Sabbath services; the very old would come each morning. They would pray together, but the magic of the holidays, the public rejoicing, was gone.

It is hard to summarize one's impressions of a trip that included so many powerful experiences, each of them a turning point in one's own life. It is hard to balance them against one another, to draw a line, add them up, point to the total, and say, "Here is the problem; here is its solution." He who has lived through the experience may laugh or cry, but he cannot define it rationally, cannot be content with a scientific or a literary interpretation, cannot build a theoretical system adequate to explain it. He may, if he has the strength left, voice a wordless scream.

In your first confrontation with the Jews of Russia you are forced to abandon whatever intellectual baggage you may have brought with you. Logic, you suddenly realize, will not help you here. You have your logic, they have theirs, and the distance between the two cannot be bridged by words. The more you see of them the surer you become that everything you have thought or known till now is worthless; here you must begin anew. This strange new world has customs and laws totally unfamiliar to you; language operates on a level you cannot hope to comprehend. You understand nothing they tell you, and when they explain, you believe nothing. You feel as though you have been propelled into a realm of the absurd; when you try to describe it, your description has the air of a harrowing scene from a Kafkaesque novel or nightmare.

But the nightmare is not yours. It's theirs.

My summary, then, must be very personal and very short. The condition of the Jews in the Soviet Union is at once more grievous and more hopeful than I had imagined.

On the one hand, the Russian authorities do everything in their power to prevent Jews from conducting their internal affairs within a recognizable organizational framework, with its own self-esteem, its own culture and folk-lore its own scale of values. But on the other hand, they do not make it possible for Jews to acculturate to non-Jewish society, a society that is prepared to accept Ukrainians, Uzbeks, and Tartars . . . but not Jews. The impression has been created that Jews are destined to be alien forever.

The Jewish reaction is natural. Since others try to prevent them from living either as Jews or as non-Jews, they decide, despite and even because of the difficulties involved, to preserve their Jewishness. This is the only way I can explain the mass gatherings of Jews in and around the synagogue on Jewish holidays. Most of them come not to pray, not out of a belief in the God of Israel or in His Torah, but out of a desire to identify with the Jewish people—about whom they know next to nothing.

I asked dozens of them, young and old alike, "Who is a Jew? What is Judaism? What makes you a Jew?" They shrugged their shoulders. The questions do not interest them. There is a time to philosophize, a time to accept the commandments of Judaism as a revelation from Sinai, and a time to ask questions. They are Jews, and that is that; the rest is unimportant. A Jew is one who feels himself a Jew.

Soviet policy with regard to the Jews is thus doubly strange; its two contradictory stratagems produce the same undesired result. Jews remain Jews.

In the central Russian republic (RSFSR), the authorities are displeased because Jews have not adapted themselves sufficiently to Russian life; they are not Russian enough. Jews interfere with the process of Russification backed by the Kremlin. Despite the many years of coexistence, there is still considerable distance between Abraham and Ivan.

In the Ukraine, in White Russia, and in Lithuania, the complaint is just the opposite. Jews are much too Russian. The local inhabitants, who have not yet abandoned their particular national heritage, regard Jews as exemplars of the evils of Russification. They accuse them of being more Russian than Russians.

There are contradictions even in the realm of Jewish life itself. How can the great fear in

which Jews live all year long be reconciled
with their joyful outbursts on the night of
Simchat Torah? How can one explain the
appearance of tens of thousands of youngsters
at the same time and place when it seems im-
probable that anyone could have organized
them? Or how understand the fact that Jewish
communists come in considerable numbers to
the "Kol Nidrei" prayer, that so many young
Jews find themselves returning to Judaism
without knowing, without having a chance to
know, anything about it? Or the mystical
attraction that Israel has for men whose parents themselves were born after the Revolution and brought up according to its principles?

These riddles are hard to solve, for the key
is not found in our brains but in our hearts. An
intellectual approach can succeed only in
clouding the issue still further. In the last
analysis, this phenomenon can be understood
only in the context of the mystery of Jewish
survival from ancient times to the present. Its
roots lie deep in the vital emotions of the
human heart, which is capable of fear even
when there seems to be no logical reason for
it. But sooner or later, the heart will be proved
right. "We are the only Jews left on earth,"
I had been told. Only they—because they have
yet to give up the dream—only they still look
for the coming of the Messiah, despite the unbearable pain that accompanies the birth of

redemption. Only they—because they have suffered more than all the rest and are worthier than all the rest of the blessing of peace and salvation. Only they—because they have remained alone.

I never heard them say that their lives in Russia were insecure. No one complained of imminent physical danger. On the contrary, compared to the hardships of the Stalin era, their present situation seems ideal. Today no one executes writers or artists for contributing their talents to Jewish culture; no one imprisons a man for speaking Yiddish on the street; if economic trials are still being held, they are no longer publicized or used to provide anti-Jewish propaganda; if there are still anti-Semites—and there are—their influence is not so strong as to create an atmosphere which might incite pogroms.

Of course, being a Jew in Russia is not the easiest or most pleasant thing in the world. Official spokesmen may deny it all they will, but not a day passed when I did not hear reports of discrimination. For a Jew to progress far enough in his career to replace a non-Jew in a given position is almost unheard of. More than feeling insecure, they feel unwanted. It is as simple as that. From all sides they are made to believe that Russia can get along quite nicely without them; in fact, that Russia without them would be a better place. And the ugly truth is that the authorities do nothing to contradict this impression.

It was in Kiev, of all places—the capital of Jewish fear—that someone dared to voice his emotions to me. "Our government is careful to tell everyone living in America or in Europe or in Israel about the wonderful contributions made by Jews to Russian culture. It stresses the fact that the great scientist, Lev Landau, is a Jew; that the economist Yevsei Lieberman is a Jew; that the violinist David Oistrakh is a Jew. Why do *we* never read about this in our papers? They do not want us to take pride in the achievements of these men; so they also 'forget' to report that Jewish officers and soldiers were among those who received the highest decorations and were proclaimed 'Heroes of the Soviet Union' in the struggle against the Germans. The world is allowed to know . . . but we are not. If we were permitted to think of them as Jews, we would one day necessarily begin to think of ourselves as Jews, too, and that cannot be allowed to happen."

What does it matter to the authorities that anti-Semites interpret this policy of silence in their own way, telling Jews that they never fought for the fatherland, never shed their blood for Russia? That all they know is business and black marketeering? That they are parasites on the nation? They say to the Jews, "If you lay in the trenches with us, why don't we know about it? If there are among you some who are known for their excellence in any field, why don't we read about it in the newspapers?"

None of this was news to me. In recent years I had heard and read a great deal about the situation of the Jews in the Soviet Union, and I knew that it was bad. I knew that Jews were in a worse position than others, that despite the progress of de-Stalinization they still enjoyed less freedom than other groups within the population. This is not what I meant when I said the situation was more grievous than I had imagined. I was referring to the Jewish fear that lurks in every pair of eyes, that makes itself felt in every conversation. It is a fear that has penetrated the cells of their bodies; it clings to them like a hateful second skin, black and solid as the night, but not so beautiful. It is the thing that cut me more deeply than anything else in my encounter with the Jews of Russia. And I still do not know whether it is justified or not. Possibly it has remained with them from the days of Stalin, but if so, many of the horrors of that period have yet to be uncovered. The general populace feels practically nothing of this fear; apparently everyone but the Jews has managed to forget those days.

The Jews alone remain bound in terror, and who can predict when, or if, they will ever be released?

I have no way of knowing whether all three million Russian Jews are haunted by this fear. I visited five cities, and in them I met only those who came to the synagogue during the High Holy Days and Sukkot, in addition to the young people who came to dance and sing in the street on the night of Simchat Torah. So I cannot truthfully assert that all the Jews in Russia live in terror, just as I cannot say that they all feel a strong attraction to the Jewish tradition. I did not meet them all, and those conversations I did manage to have were not conducted in the manner of a formal interview. For understandable reasons and because of objective difficulties, I was not able to choose my interlocutors or even to assure myself that they formed a reliable cross section of the various branches and communities of the Jewish population as a whole.

During my stay in Russia I saw tens of thousands of Jews, and I spoke to several hundred at least. However, I met almost all of them in the same place and under the same conditions . . . in and around the synagogue. And almost all our conversations were brief and fortuitous, unplanned, carried on through an elaborate system of allusion and insinuation. To be perfectly fair, then, I should note that it is almost entirely on these meetings that my impressions are based. It could be that they do not represent the views of those I failed to meet. It is possible that those who did not cross my path do not want to know about Judaism—theirs or anyone else's—that they are not interested in the state of Israel or their Jewish heritage. Everything is possible, but this is unlikely. If the air is unfriendly in Russia, it is unfriendly to them all. If there is an active system of discrimination, it discriminates against them all. And if one reacts in a certain way, it is hard to see why others would not also.

I should add that I did manage to talk fleetingly with Jews outside the synagogue, in restaurants and airports, hotels and trains. Not one of them had anything to say which contradicted what I had heard from the others. Not one of them failed to express his pain, whether by his silence, or a twisted smile, or through words that managed to hide more than they revealed. Jews who did not look like Jews, Jews who had perhaps concealed their Jewishness for a long time, somehow felt the need to identify themselves to me, another Jew.

Before I left for the Soviet Union I determined that the purpose of my trip was to discover if the Jews of Russia really wanted to be Jews. I never imagined that the answer would be so absolute and clear. I could never have foreseen that I would stand in a synagogue surrounded by men of all ages, not only the old; that I would be present at a public gathering of thirty thousand youngsters on the night of Simchat Torah and that they would be singing in Hebrew and Yiddish. Who would have thought that teenagers would be dancing the *hora* on a Moscow street, shouting "David, King of Israel, lives and endures"? Who could have dreamed that some of them—perhaps many of them—would be studying the Hebrew language, would be passing slips of paper back and forth covered with Hebrew words?

On that night of Simchat Torah I happened to be in the company of a Jew from abroad who prided himself on his antireligious and antinationalist convictions, a cold, dry, unsentimental, liberated Jew. The youngsters were singing, "Come let us go together, all of us together, and greet the Jewish people." Unable to contain himself, he burst into tears. The next day he appeared at the synagogue. "Don't think I've become religious," he said to me. "It's not that. But they have made me a better Jew."

Who knows—perhaps our salvation, too, will come from them.

While in Russia I heard two stories about Soviet Jews which indicated the indomitable strength of their convictions. The first concerned an act of communal heroism, the second an example of individual piety. Both stories came to me, as one says, from highly reliable sources.

In a city somewhere in Georgia, the authorities decided to raze the synagogue and use the site for a new Komsomol club. The Jews were ordered to evacuate the building, which they were told had become too old and dilapidated to be used any longer. Their devotion to the synagogue was such that they offered to raise the necessary funds among themselves to build the club elsewhere, if they could be allowed to keep their building. The offer was refused, and in desperate resolve the Jews decided to resist. The workers who arrived with bulldozers to begin clearing the site found them lying down to block the street that led to the synagogue. Men, women, and children, they absolutely refused to move. The authorities were not eager to start a riot. The workers left; the decision to destroy the synagogue was revoked.

The second incident also took place in Georgia, were Jews were known for their defiant stand even during the "black days" of Stalin.

One morning there was a knock at the door of a man who for some years had secretly and at great risk brought dozens of children into the covenant of Abraham. His wife opened the door, and was confronted by a Russian colonel. "Does Comrade K . . . live here?" Terrified, she answered yes. The officer demanded to speak to her husband. "I have heard that you are a *mohel;* true or not?" The man tried to deny it. "Don't waste your breath." The officer commanded the man to get dressed; his wife packed his personal belongings in a satchel. "Take your 'instruments,' " the colonel ordered.

They got into an army vehicle, and the man was blindfolded. They rode for about half an hour, then got out; the colonel opened a door and removed the blindfold. They were standing in a well-furnished apartment. A woman lay in bed, a crib by her side. "You must circumcise my son," the colonel said. The ceremony took five minutes. The father asked the price, but the *mohel* refused to take money. The colonel would not hear of it. He gave the man 25 rubles and two bottles of vodka, blindfolded him again, and drove him home.

I do not know whether similar incidents take place every day, in every city or in every family. Perhaps they do—perhaps not. It is possible that not all Jews want or are prepared to circumcise their sons or to fight for their synagogues. But there *are* Jews who will under no circumstances let themselves be severed from their people.

That is what I wanted to see, and that is what I saw. It is good for us to know; it is essential that we know, both for them and for ourselves. No matter how often it is repeated, the official claim that, apart from a few old men, the majority of Russian Jews wish to forget their Jewish identity is simply untrue.

One of the last Jews I met in Moscow was a rabbinical scholar. In comparing the present situation to that of the recent past, he quoted to me the commentary given by Rabbi Menachem Mendel of Kotzk to a verse from Exodus, "And the king of Egypt died, and the children of Israel sighed by reason of their bondage." The question was raised: All the time Pharaoh was alive the Jews labored and suffered; why, then, did they sigh at his death? Rabbi Menachem Mendel answered that before Pharaoh died, even to sigh had been forbidden. "Do you understand?" the scholar said. "Today we are permitted to sigh . . . although only when no one is listening."

That the Jews in the free world do not heed this sigh will never be forgiven them. Of that I am sure. For the second time in a single generation, we are committing the error of silence.

One may question whether we have any way of knowing that the Jews of Russia really want us to do anything for them. How do we know that our shouts and protests will not bring them harm? These are very serious questions, and I put them to the Russian Jews themselves. Their answer was always the same: "Cry out, cry out until you have no more strength to cry. You must enlist public opinion, you must turn to those with influence, you must involve your governments—the hour is late."

In Kiev a Jew said to me, "I hope you will not have cause to regret that you have abandoned us." And in Moscow a religious Jew said, "The preservation of human life takes precedence over all six hundred thirteen commandments. Don't you know that? Don't our cries reach you? Or do they reach you but not move you? If that is so, then we are truly lost, because you live in a world wholly guilty, and your hearts have become foul." In every city I heard dozens of cries like these, almost without variation. I was not to forget, I was to tell it all, I was to warn the Jewish communities of the world that their continued indifference would be accounted a horrible crime in the years to come. I promised I would do it, but I wept before them as I promised. I wept because I knew that nothing would help. Our Jews have other problems on their minds. When you tell them what is expected of them in Russia, they shrug their shoulders. It is exaggerated; or, we can do nothing about it; or, we must not do too much lest we be accused of interfering in the cold war. The Jewish brain has killed the Jewish heart. That is why I wept.

I believe with all my soul that despite the suffering, despite the hardship and the fear, the Jews of Russia will withstand the pressure and emerge victorious. But whether or not we shall ever be worthy of their trust, whether or not we shall overcome the pressures we have ourselves created, I cannot say. I returned from the Soviet Union disheartened and depressed. But what torments me most is not the Jews of silence I met in Russia, but the silence of the Jews I live among today.

Historical
Afterword
on
Soviet Jewry
by Neal Kozodoy

There are, according to the official Soviet census of 1959, some 2,268,000 Jews now living in the Soviet Union.[1] Of these, the largest proportion (75 per cent) resides in the Russian and Ukrainian republics; the rest are scattered throughout the remaining thirteen republics, with sizable communities in Byelorussia, Uzbekistan, Georgia, Lithuania, Moldavia, Latvia, and Estonia. They are concentrated heavily (95 per cent) in urban areas. All in all, the Jews form a small minority, 1.09 per cent of the total Soviet population.

Like the Ukrainians, Georgians, Germans,

[1] The exact figure, as reported in *Pravda*, February 4, 1960, was 2,267,814. However, there are reasons to believe that the actual number is closer to 3,000,000, since for the first time registrants were not required to provide proof of nationality and many Jews, particularly those married to non-Jews, may well have declared their nationality to be other than that specified on their internal passport. See Moshe Decter, "The Status of the Jews in the Soviet Union," in *Foreign Affairs*, January, 1963, and William Korey, "The Legal Position of the Jews in the Soviet Union," in *Midstream*, May, 1966. I wish particularly to thank Moshe Decter for sharing generously with me the results of his own extensive research into the problem of the Jews in the Soviet Union.

and so forth, Jews are regarded by Soviet law as members of a distinct nationality, despite the fact that they lack a continuous geographic territory. Under the terms of a decree first issued in 1932, every Soviet citizen is required to have his nationality specified on his "internal passport," the principal means of identification in the USSR.[2] Thus, a person born of Jewish parents is automatically listed as Jewish. (One born of mixed parentage may, upon registering, select as his own the nationality of either parent.)

As a nationality Jews are entitled to rights guaranteed by law and extending to the free development of their culture and their language. Yiddish (Hebrew, as a language of liturgy, was from the earliest day of the Soviet regime considered reactionary and an instrument of Zionism and was effectively suppressed). Up until 1948, with a few brief interruptions, Jews enjoyed a cultural life of their own, with newspapers, books, and journals, publishing houses, schools, professional theaters, and research institutions. Today, despite USSR ratification of the 1962 UNESCO Convention against Discrimination in Education, which obligates it "to recognize the right of

[2] Decree adopted by the Central Executive Committee and the Council of Peoples' Commissars, December 27, 1932. (*Pravda*, December 28, 1932)

members of national minorities to carry on
their own educational activities, including the
maintenance of school and . . . the use or the
teaching of their own language,"[3] there is not a
single Yiddish school throughout the Soviet
Union nor a single class where Yiddish is
taught. (In the 1959 census, 18 per cent of
those registered as Jews—a little over 400,000
—gave Yiddish as their native language, although here, too, the actual figures of those
who read or speak the language are probably
higher than the official report indicates.) By
way of contrast, the Volga Germans, who like
the Jews are dispersed over several territories
and whose total number (according to the
1959 census) comes to somewhat over 1,600,-
000, have, since their restoration to national
rights in 1964, enjoyed the full benefit of
schools, textbooks, and pedagogical institutions. "In districts of a number of provinces,
territories and republics that have a German
population, there are secondary and elementary schools where teaching is conducted in

[3] Commission on Human Rights, "Study of Discrimination in Education," January 5, 1961. See also the statement made by the Soviet government to UNESCO: "The
Union of the Soviet Socialist Republics reports that every
Soviet citizen may have his children taught in any language he wishes. . . ." (Commission on Human Rights,
"Periodic Reports on Human Rights Covering the Period
1960-1962," December 20, 1963.)

German or German is taught to children of school age. . . ."[4]

The closing of Jewish schools after World War II was followed by the dismantlement of the large Jewish publishing structure. The publishing house Der Emes (The Truth), which had brought out the thrice-weekly *Aynikayt* and 110 other publications in the three years after the war, was closed in 1948, its fonts of Yiddish type melted down. The Jewish State Theater in Moscow was shut down in 1949, about a year after its leading actor, the legendary Solomon Mikhoels, was murdered by the secret police. The Jewish Anti-fascist Committee, of which Mikhoels had been an official, was dissolved in 1948, and most of its other officials were also liquidated.

In 1959, six years after Stalin's death, the first Yiddish book, by Sholom Aleichem, appeared after a silence of eleven years. It was followed by four more Yiddish books written by deceased authors. In 1962 and 1963, no Yiddish books were published. More appeared in 1964, with promises of still more to come. (In 1961 alone, by comparison, 62 books were produced in the Soviet Union for the Maris and 144 for the Yakuts in their own languages. The Maris and Yakuts are two small, primitive

---

[4] From a decree of the Presidium of the USSR Supreme Soviet, signed on August 29, 1964, published December 28, 1964.

Asian groups, numbering 504,000 and 236,000 respectively.[5] In 1964, two Yiddish books were published in a total of 18,000 copies. The Maris that year had 56 books published in their own language in a total of 180,000 copies.) There is still no Yiddish theater, with the exception of traveling groups of amateur actors and singers. (The Gypsies, numbering 132,-000, have a state theater.) Nor is there any newspaper, except for the *Birobidzhaner Shtern* (Birobidzhan Star), a triweekly paper produced in the Jewish Autonomous Region of Birobidzhan (whose 14,000 Jews comprise 8.8 per cent of the region's population), in an edition of 1,000, containing mostly local news and translations of items from the major papers.[6] In 1961, a Yiddish literary journal, *Sovietish Heimland* (Soviet Homeland) began publication as a bimonthly, with a press run of 25,000, a sizable proportion of which was marked for shipment abroad. At the time, Yekaterina Furtseva, the Soviet Minister of

[5] Moshe Decter, "Status of the Jews."

[6] The Jewish Autonomous Region of Birobidzhan in the Far East was established by decree of the Presidium of the Central Executive Committee of the USSR in 1934, and was recommended as a "national homeland" for Soviet Jews. Relatively few were attracted there as permanent residents, and today, as former Premier Khrushchev noted in an interview printed in the French newspaper *Le Figaro*, April 9, 1958, "All that is left now in Birobidzhan are signs in Yiddish at the railroad station, but there are no Jews. . . ."

Culture, declared that the decision to allow publication of the Yiddish journal was taken "to please our friends abroad."[7] *Sovietish Heimland* is now a monthly journal, and has published the work of over 100 Jewish authors. Its editor, Aron Vergelis, vigorously denies the presence of discrimination in the Soviet Union against Jewish national culture, despite the fact that the Jewish writers and artists purged in the "black years" under Stalin have yet to be formally rehabilitated as a group.

More than a nationality, Jews in the Soviet Union are also considered to be a religious group, and as such are subject to the campaign against all religion conducted by the Communist Party. The state, however, as distinguished from the party, guarantees the right of all religious citizens to worship freely.[8] This includes the right to organize central federative bodies, such as the Holy Synod of the Russian Orthodox Church, the All-Union Council of Evangelical Christian-Baptists, the Moslem Board, and so forth. Judaism, however, has not had a central coordinating body since 1926. It is unable to publish periodicals or devotional literature, manufacture ritual ob-

[7] *Jerusalem Post*, February 3, 1961.
[8] Decree of the Council of Peoples' Commissars of January 23, 1918, subsequently reiterated. See, too, the report of the Soviet government to the United Nations, available in "Study of Discrimination in the Matter of Religious Rights and Practices, Conference Room Paper No. 35."

jects, maintain training schools for rabbis, or enjoy formal contacts with coreligionists abroad.

In 1959, fifty thousand copies of the Russian Orthodox version of the Bible were released by state-owned presses. In 1958, the Baptists issued a Russian edition of the Protestant Bible in ten thousand copies. Even though the state has assured all religions lacking federative centers a supply of "necessary paper and the use of printing plants,"[9] no Hebrew Bible has been published in the Soviet Union since 1917, and no Jewish religious book of any other kind has appeared in print since the 1920's. In 1957, a photo-offset reproduction of a pre-revolutionary *siddur* (prayerbook) was permitted in an edition of three thousand copies. Religious calendars are unavailable, except for photographed copies of handwritten calendars that circulate from hand to hand. Similarly, devotional articles such as the *talith* (prayer shawl) and *tfilin* (phylacteries) are virtually impossible to obtain.

The Russian Orthodox Church maintains two academies and five seminaries for the training of priests; the Moslems have a *madrassa* in Russia, and in addition are allowed to send their clerical students abroad to the seminary in Cairo. The Jews had no institution for the training of rabbis until 1957, when a Yeshivah

[9] "Conference Room Paper 35," p. 14.

(rabbinical academy) was established at the Great Synagogue in Moscow. Since that time it has ordained two students. Of the thirteen who were studying at the Yeshivah in April 1962—eleven of them over the age of forty —nine were prevented from resuming their studies in Moscow on grounds that they lacked the permits necessary for residence in the capital. According to the New York *Times* of July 27, 1965, the chief rabbi, Yehuda-Leib Levin, told an American delegation of rabbis that the government would permit twenty students to register in the Yeshivah in the fall of that year. Needless to say, Jewish rabbinical students are not allowed to pursue their course of study abroad. Nor has any Jewish religious delegation from the USSR been permitted to visit Jewish institutions outside the Soviet Union or to maintain formal ties with co-religionists abroad. During the Jewish High Holy Days in September, 1961, a special loge was constructed in the Great Synagogue of Moscow for the seating of visitors and officials from the Israel Embassy to prevent communication between local worshipers and foreigners. In October, 1961, lay leaders of the Moscow and Leningrad synagogues, among them Gedaliah Pecharsky of Leningrad, were convicted of alleged espionage and sentenced to lengthy prison terms for conspiring with "Israeli spies," who were in turn described as tools of American intelligence.[10]

In 1957, restrictions were passed on the public baking and sale of matzah, the unleavened bread eaten by religious Jews during Passover. At first the ban was confined to the city of Kharkov, but it soon spread to other areas. In March, 1962, Rabbi Levin announced that the public baking and sale of matzah were totally forbidden—the machines in the state bakery had "broken down"—and he advised his congregants to bake an unleavened bread at home. Passover of 1963 saw no change in the situation, but in July, 1963, four Jews were brought to trial on charges of profiteering in the production and sale of matzah. In the meantime the authorities changed their position and now claimed that it was illegal for state bakeries to produce matzah or for state stores to sell it on the grounds of separation of church and state. In a document submitted to the United Nations on July 11, 1956, however, Soviet policy had been spelled out as follows:

By order of the USSR Government, on days preceding particularly important holidays—such as Passover in the case of the Jews —the shops of the state trading organizations

[10] *Trud*, January, 1962.

sell special types of bakery products, matzah for Orthodox Jews, etc., to enable worshipers to perform the appropriate ritual.[11]

In 1964, the Moscow Jewish community was permitted to rent a small bakery for the production of matzah, and Rabbi Levin was also authorized to request shipments from abroad, although many of these were subsequently impounded or returned by the authorities. By 1965, in response to protests from abroad, some synagogues were allowed to produce matzah on their own premises. A Jew desiring to obtain the unleavened bread must bring the necessary flour to the synagogue and register his identity, a procedure which leaves much to be desired and is in any case only a step toward restoring the status quo as it was before 1957, when matzah was freely available in state stores throughout the country.[12]

Ever since the Bolshevik seizure of power in November, 1917, the Soviet government has consistently reaffirmed the civil rights of Russian citizens and taken legal measures to punish any infringements of those rights. Discrimination on grounds of race or creed was to be eradicated in all areas of life, especially

[11] "Conference Room Paper 35," p. 11.

[12] See "Passover and Matzoth: A Case History of Soviet Policy," Commission Study presented at the Ad Hoc Commission on the Rights of Soviet Jews, Carnegie International Center, New York, March 18, 1966.

those pertaining to such matters as residence and movement, employment, schooling, military service, ownership and use of property, and participation in elections and government. In a number of these areas, Jews do in fact

enjoy the civil rights spelled out in the legal statutes. Residential restrictions are non-existent, and there are no barriers to participation in various aspects of social life—the Party, trade unions, army, social services, clubs. Employment opportunities in a number of fields—particularly in science, medicine, law and the arts—are widespread.[13]

Nevertheless, it has become increasingly apparent that Jews are now subject to discriminatory employment practices in various administrative bureaus of the government and that quota restrictions operate with regard to Jews in party leadership positions and in education. In an interview held by a parliamentary delegation of the French Socialist Party on May 12, 1956, former Premier Nikita Khrushchev said:

Our heterogeneous populations have their republics. . . . Each of them has an autonomous government. Formerly backward and illiterate, these peoples now have their engineers and professionals. . . .

[13] William Korey, "Legal Position of the Jews."

Anti-Semitic sentiments still exist there. They are remnants of a reactionary past. This is a complicated problem because of the position of the Jews and their relations with other peoples. At the outset of the Revolution, we had many Jews in the leadership of the Party and State. They were more educated, maybe more revolutionary than the average Russian. In due course we have created new cadres. . . .

Should the Jews want to occupy the foremost positions in our republics now, it would naturally be taken amiss by the indigenous inhabitants. The latter would ill receive these pretensions, especially as they do not consider themselves less intelligent nor less capable than the Jews.[14]

This attitude, in which Jews are regarded as alien pretenders rather than as members of the "indigenous" population of the Soviet Union, was reasserted by Soviet officials in subsequent interviews, and the practice of excluding Jews from certain key positions has apparently continued.[15] However, internal Soviet reaction to this unofficial policy of dis-

[14] *Réalités*, May, 1957.

[15] See the interview with Yekaterina Furtseva in the *National Guardian*, June 25, 1956, and the articles by J. B. Salsberg, the former Canadian communist leader, in *Vochenblatt* and *Morgen Freiheit*, October through December, 1956; also Salsberg's article, "Anti-Semitism in the USSR?" in *Jewish Life*, February, 1957. None of these interviews was reported in the Soviet press.

crimination is now beginning to be expressed. Konstantin Skriabin, a Soviet academician, indirectly alluded to discriminatory practices at a meeting of the Central Committee in March, 1962: "From my point of view," he said, "a scientist should not be evaluated by his passport but by his head, from the point of view of his ability and social usefulness."[16] And an editorial in Pravda on September 5, 1965, after attacking for the first time in over two decades manifestations of anti-Semitism, went on to note:

It is necessary to remember that the growing scale of Communist construction requires a constant exchange of cadres among the peoples. Therefore any manifestations of national separateness in the training and employment of personnel of various nationalities in the Soviet Republics are intolerable.

The proportion of Jews in political life has also been declining for many years. In 1937, 32 of the 569 deputies in the Supreme Soviet, 5.6 per cent, were Jews, whereas in the current Supreme Soviet only 8 of the 1,517 members are Jews, 0.5 per cent. Of the Supreme Soviets of the 15 Union republics, only in Lithuania does Jewish representation correspond to Jewish population figures, and al-

[16] *Pravda*, March 8, 1962.

though the Novosti Press Agency (*Jews in the Soviet Union*, 1963) has publicized the figure of 7,623 Jews elected to local Soviets in 1961, it neglected to note that the total number of members elected that year came to 1,823,049. Jewish representation thus stands at about 0.4 per cent, as compared to the figure of 1.09 per cent in the total population. A study of Jewish representation in leadership positions of the Communist Party reveals similar discrepancies.[17]

Nicholas DeWitt, an American specialist on Soviet education, has noted that the quota system in admissions policies of universities operates "to the particularly severe disadvantage of the Jewish population."[18] In 1935 Jews represented 13.5 per cent of all students in higher education, a figure which dropped by the end of 1960 to 3.2 per cent, although during the same period the Jewish proportion of the population decreased only from 1.6 to 1.2 per cent. Furthermore, "in those republics where Jews constitute an above average proportion of the urban population, their representation among university students is well below higher education."[19] It should be noted,

[17] William Korey, "Legal Position of the Jews."

[18] *Education and Professional Employment in the USSR*, Washington, 1961.

[19] Nicholas DeWitt, "The Status of Jews in Soviet Education," mimeographed, 1964.

too, that Soviet statistics on "higher education" combine in one category universities and other types of specialized schools, such as teacher training institutions and music conservatories. Jews are heavily represented in the latter types of school, and "this fact artificially raises the total by balancing out the much lower proportion of Jews in the universities as such."[20]

The actual situation of the Jews in the Soviet Union must be seen against the background of a consistent campaign by the press and other official organs to denigrate the Jewish national character and the Jewish religion. Much of this campaign, in its language and direction, seems to be a carry-over from the darkest years of Stalin's reign of terror (1948–1953), when Jewish artists and writers were characterized as "homeless cosmopolitans" and were systematically liquidated. This period culminated in the notorious "Doctors' Plot" affair, in which prominent doctors were indicted as agents of an American-Zionist conspiracy, allegedly masterminded by the Joint Distribution Committee, to murder Soviet leaders. Only Stalin's death in 1953 saved these men from execution or banishment, and the whole affair was subsequently denounced as a sham, a "violation of Socialist legality."

[20] Moshe Decter, "Status of the Jews."

In newspaper articles today, Jews figure prominently as examples of antisocial types, profiteers, and conspirators. They are frequently singled out for mention in articles dealing with more general social ills, where, in a continuation of an old Stalinist policy, their Russian names are stripped away and their Semitic first names and patronymics given in full. A rather mild example of such news items appeared in *Trud*, the Soviet Trade Union paper, on June 9, 1963, over the signature of N. Ehrlich, the *Trud* "expert" on Jewish affairs. The text is in full:

In Vladimir Dal's dictionary the verb "to cling" is construed as "to attach oneself," "to harass," "to bother." The corresponding noun "clinger" [hanger-on] is construed by Dal as "a bore," "one who won't move away," "a man who foists himself upon others."

These epithets alone do not exactly evoke deep respect for the man thus characterized. There are, however, people who even take pride in this "calling," who make clinging their profession. We speak of hangers-on and loafers. They can often be seen in the central squares of our cities, in hotels, at receptions of certain foreign embassies. In other words, wherever one can meet foreigners.

The Soviet public has nothing but contempt for loafers; they are people alien to us. In our country all possibilities have been created for productive labor. Every citizen of the Soviet Union has the opportunity to work not out of need but following his heart's command. Unfortunately there are still in our country people who try to live at the expense of others, to live as parasites. Finding no sympathy among honest toilers, these hangers-on and loafers attach themselves to foreigners, who throw miserable pittances their way in return for a vulgar joke or lampoon at the expense of our reality—from torn socks to the daubing of abstractionists. Take, O Lord, what we can afford [Russian proverb].

It has somehow developed that whenever one talks of "hangers-on" the image of some "stylyaga" [beatnik] comes to one's mind, complete with a shaggy mop of hair and ultra narrow trousers. It is not all that correct. There are "hangers-on" who, even more aggravating, are of a very, very respectable age —fathers of families.

Here you have three of them. Get acquainted: Moisie Lvovich Chernukhin, born 1907, Zinoviy Isaakovich Roginsky, born 1897, and Shimon Avseyavich Sheyfer, born 1883. They cling to foreign tourists and certain embassies in Moscow. It is unpleasant even to discuss them, but we are duty bound to speak about them as people have been coming to our Editorial Office to complain indignantly about the unsavory conduct of these individuals who have lost all sense of shame and conscience. Let their dirty little deals become public property.

As far back as 1949, Chernukhin, along with other characters of his type, had been telling spurious tales about the conditions of life in our country. This calumny was used by the Israeli press to fan a hostile campaign against the Soviet Union.

In subsequent years Chernukhin many times met with Israeli citizens, obtaining from them Zionist and religious literature as well as items of religious observance. But do not think this was because of an ardent belief in God. The *taliths* [ritual shawls for prayer— N.E.], for instance, he used to sell to believers at speculative prices.

This hanger-on of declining years just loves embassy receptions. It is a passionate love, and he tries not to miss out on a single one. This love of his led him, a semiliterate, hardly able to read or write, to a reception at the Israeli Embassy held in honor of writers, artists, and scientists who came from Israel to Moscow to attend the World Congress for Universal Disarmament and Peace. Not conversation on methods of literary and scientific development occupied Chernukhin on that evening. Creeping like a snake from one foreigner to another, he begged for knick-knacks, surreptitiously stuffing his pockets and lining his clothes with little booklets of dubious contents which were lavishly strewn on the tables. He did not by-pass oranges and sweets, either. He swiped everything.

Chernukhin does not omit holding out his palms for considerations to foreigners in the Moscow Choral Synagogue. One could see him often enough, not having finished his prayers, plunging headlong to the exit of the synagogue to lie in wait for foreigners.

Chernukhin's conduct evokes righteous indignation on the part of the believing habitués. At their demand he was expelled from the so-called "Committee of Twenty" [the governing body of the synagogue—N.E.], which deprived Chernukhin of the means to mingle with foreign guests, but this did not stop the ardent hanger-on. He manages to squeeze into the synagogue by the back door for a cringing handshake with foreigners, at the same time wheedling something for his speculatory machinations.

His visits to embassies are dictated by a determination to grab as much foreign knickknacks and foreign literature as possible with the aim of speculation.

A characteristic instance. On October 17, 1962, the Israeli Embassy organized a reception on the occasion of the Jewish New Year. Of course, Roginsky was there. The guests were talking and exchanging news while Roginsky was skipping around the tables, well-stocked with *taliths*, prayer books, books, journals, records, postcards, etc. The longer he skipped around these tables the thicker his pockets got, and the wider swelled his sides. Toward the end of the reception Roginsky had grown so "obese" that one could hardly recognize him.

Sheyfer prefers to "work" at the synagogue. He spends all his free time there, and that he has in abundance. He is an old-age pensioner. Suffice it for a foreigner to show his face at the synagogue—Sheyfer is right there at his side begging for *taliths*, literature, and overseas knickknacks. The more the better.

Just a short while ago, on June 1, Sheyfer (for the umpteenth time) became the hero of a scandalous incident. During the service at Choral Synagogue, he sneaked into the box where the foreigners were sitting and started begging for "souvenirs." A member of the congregation, Rabinovich, told him off. In answer to this, such a torrent of abuse poured out of Sheyfer's lips that even an edited version of it would be too indecent to print. Sheyfer was running amok to such an extent that members of the congregation were compelled to throw him out of doors.

One could supply many more facts about the conduct of Chernukhin, Roginsky, and Sheyfer, but even from what has already been said it is clear how low these far-from-young people have fallen. Hangers-on like Chernukhin, Roginsky, Sheyfer, and the likes of them do not act out of friendly feelings toward foreigners nor out of a desire to help

them to know our country and the life of the
Soviet people better. Avarice, groveling ser-
vility before everything foreign, spiritual
waste, lack of pride in our great motherland
—these impel the Chernukhins, Roginskys,
and the Sheyfers into the embraces of sometimes not entirely blameless foreigners.

A few words addressed to those who are
palsy-walsy with such hangers-on.

Every year more and more Soviet people
go abroad, more and more foreigners visit
the Soviet Union. We have no intention at all
to conceal ourselves from them with a stone
wall. But we have our own Soviet pride. We
do not like to breathe the same air with
hangers-on and loafers, to be with them in
the same room. Foreigners should never forget it if they really want to have true friends
among Soviet citizens.[21]

Countless such articles appear every year,
in major newspapers like *Pravda*, *Izvestia*, and
Trud, as well as in local papers. Although the
names and circumstances differ, the character-
ization of Jews remains constant. They are
uniformly depicted as marginal men, parasites
on the Soviet economy, sneaky and "snake-
like" in their movements, seeking out "not
entirely blameless" foreigners for the purpose
of maligning the Soviet homeland and gaining
small trinkets and devotional articles which

---

[21] Quoted from *Jews in Eastern Europe*, September, 1963.

they later sell at exorbitant prices. Hints of conspiracy with Israeli embassy officials are common. While some of these newspaper articles seem to be gratuitously insulting, others are directed at a clear goal. For example, the virulent press campaign conducted in Lvov from February to November, 1962, finally resulted in the closing of the Great Synagogue of Lvov, the last Jewish house of prayer in that Ukrainian city.[22] Indeed, the campaign against the Jewish religion has had the effect of reducing the number of synagogues in the Soviet Union from a mere 450 in 1956 to 96 by April, 1963, and to 60 by the summer of 1965. Jews are consistently portrayed as visiting the synagogue for the sole purpose of dealing in black-market goods and engaging in anti-Soviet espionage activities.

Very often, charges against the Jewish religion are linked to themes of ideological subversion and political disloyalty on the part of Jews, especially their alleged subversive ties with the state of Israel. The Soviet Union, in 1948, was the first country in the world to extend formal recognition to Israel, but this initial overture was abruptly followed by a policy of hostility. Attacks by the press often

[22] For an analysis and excerpts from the Soviet press, see Moshe Decter, "The Lvov Case: A Self-Portrait of Soviet Anti-Semitism," *Midstream*, June, 1963.

concern themselves with the holiday of Passover and its supposed message of nationalistic
independence which is exploited by "Zionist
conspirators":

> The peculiar characteristic of most Jewish
> holidays is their clear expression of national-
> ism. Such festivals as Passover, for example,
> give rise to nationalist feelings, and poison
> the minds of Jews by diverting their thoughts
> to Israel, "the land of their fathers." . . .
> Judaism kills love for the Soviet mother-
> land.[23]

> Jewish bourgeois organizations are doing
> their utmost to revive Judaism in our circum-
> stances. Many Israeli tourists disseminate Zi-
> onist literature. Every year the Minsk syna-
> gogue receives matzah packages from abroad.
> But the matter doesn't stop at these "gifts"
> alone. Judaism is trying to create an ideologi-
> cal subversion, to fill the consciousness of
> working Jews in our country with bourgeois
> ideology.[24]

One key phrase that occurs time and again

[23] F. S. Mayatsky in *Sovietskaya Moldavia*, official daily
government newspaper in Kishinev, capital of Moldavia,
July 23, 1959.

[24] From "The Shadow of the Synagogue," by J. Muraviev,
in *Zviazda*, the leading Byelorussian-language paper of
Minsk, capital of the Byelorussian republic, February 2,
1965. For an appraisal of Soviet-Israel relations see "Israel
in the Soviet Mirror," a special issue of *Jews in Eastern
Europe*, December, 1965.

in Soviet portrayals of Jews is that of "the golden calf." Jews are depicted as eagerly debasing themselves in a frantic search for profit, and the scene of their nefarious activities is frequently the synagogue:

> For these "saints" nothing is holy! But there is one thing they consider holy: Money, money, money. . . . And the flow comes through into the pockets of the parasites of the Jewish synagogue of Alma Ata.
> Money—this is their ideal. . . . This spring, Fanya Weisman and Sioma Weiner began to bake matzah. Were they motivated by religious feelings? Oh no! They wanted to profit from believers.
> Stuffing themselves with matzoth and ethrogim, the preachers of Judaism—Spector, Kotlaryevsky, Shuchat, and Monastryrsky—pray only to the golden calf: how to collect more money from the believers for their own needs and for the militant spirit of the Israeli militarists.
> The gods of the servitors of the synagogue are profit and money—"the golden calf."[25]

The campaign to discredit Jews and Judaism reached a climax of a sort during the economic trials held in the Soviet Union from 1961 to 1965, which saw the reintroduction of capital

[25] Quoted in "Passover and Matzoth: A Case History of Soviet Policy."

punishment for crimes like embezzlement, bribery, and currency speculation. (Contrary to first reports, it now appears that the sentences were indeed carried out.) Thousands of persons were arrested, tried, and convicted to the accompaniment of sweeping press coverage and notoriety. Of the more than 200 sentenced to death, about 55 per cent were Jews, and in the Ukraine 80 per cent were Jews. The press campaign focused almost exclusively and with extraordinary zeal on the Jewish malefactors, and the reports reaching the West soon elicited a wave of protest, highlighted by Bertrand Russell's appeal to Premier Khrushchev for an amnesty.[26] A study of the economic trials carried out by the International Commission of Jurists concluded:

There has been an insidious and sometimes subtle propaganda campaign directed against the Jewish people of the Soviet Union, specifically against those charged with economic crimes and also against the supposed general characteristics of Jews that have been reiterated for centuries. If the reports of trials for economic crimes are even reasonably complete, the number of Jews receiving death sentences and severe terms of imprisonment is greatly disproportionate to their number as a minority group. . . .

[26] *Pravda* and *Izvestia*, February 28, 1963.

There is undoubtedly also a certain amount of anti-Semitic prejudice at all levels of Soviet society. . . . It is a simple matter to link the picture of the money-grubbing Jew of anti-Semitic fancy with the picture of the archvillains of capitalist cupidity. This had certainly been done by the Soviet press, but the most that can safely be said is that the picture painted of the moral malaise in the Soviet Union diverts attention toward Jews because the primary object of the Soviet polity is to divert attention away from the real truth, to find scapegoats. . . . It is a tragedy for the Soviet Jewish people that they have been made the scapegoat for the transgressions of those whose guilt it would be dangerous to make public.[27]

Apprehension over Soviet treatment of Jews turned into outrage in February, 1964, when news reached the West of the publication of an anti-Semitic tract by the Ukrainian Academy of Sciences in Kiev. The book was *Judaism without Embellishment*, written by Professor Trofim Kichko, a Ukrainian academic "specialist" on Jews and Judaism. It was published in an edition of twelve thousand copies as a "scientific" study and work of scholarship,

[27] "Economic Crimes in the Soviet Union," in *Journal of the International Commission of Jurists*, Summer, 1964. See also Moshe Decter, "Soviet Justice and the Jews," *Midstream*, March, 1965.

with the following imprimatur from the Academy of Sciences:

> There is no doubt that the profound and substantial work by T. K. Kichko, which contains a tremendous amount of factual material conscientiously and scientifically analyzed, will be a valuable manual for propagandists of atheism in their daily work and will assist wide circles of readers to appraise questions regarding the Jewish religion.[28]

The contents of the 192-page volume are familiar enough. The book asserts that Judaism teaches contempt for workers and peasants, glorifies usury and extortion, and leads its adherents into hypocrisy, bribery, and financial speculation. Judaism "is impregnated with narrow practicality, with greed, the love of money, and the spirit of egoism." The book further connects Judaism with a worldwide conspiracy of Zionism and Western capitalism.

The text of *Judaism without Embellishment* is illustrated with a series of vicious cartoons sharply reminiscent of Nazi propaganda caricatures of the type found in Julius Streicher's *Der Stuermer*. They depict hooknosed Jews, wearing phylacteries, in the act of confiscating synagogue funds or brawling in the synagogue

---

[28] See Moshe Decter, "The Soviet Book That Shook the Communist World," *Midstream*, June, 1964.

over the distribution of spoils won from speculation in matzah and pigs and from thievery,
deception, and debauchery. Ben-Gurion is
seen "at work," erasing the word "not" from
the Commandments, "Thou shalt not lie [*sic*],"
"Thou shalt not murder," "Thou shalt not
steal"; another cartoon, captioned "Bonn-
Gurion," shows the ghost of Auschwitz trying to restrain the former premier of Israel
from signing a document entitled, "An Agree-
ment to Supply Arms to the Bundeswehr," a
reference to the alleged military alliance between Israel and West Germany. Another
illustration depicts a servile Jew licking a
gigantic Nazi Storm Trooper boot, in allusion
to the frequent Soviet assertion that during
the years of the Hitlerite occupation, Zionist
leaders served the Nazis and collaborated in
their plans.

The publication of *Judaism without Embellishment* provoked an unprecedented storm
of world-wide protest, most notably on the
part of Jewish and general communist movements in Western Europe, Latin America,
Australia, and the United States. For the first
time, Soviet authorities found it necessary to
issue a public disavowal. The book was criticized, with certain qualifications, by the Ideological Commission of the Central Committee
of the Soviet Communist Party, and this criti-

cism was published in the Soviet press.[29] According to various reports, the remaining copies of the book were apparently seized and destroyed.[30]

The "Kichko Affair" did much to mobilize public opinion outside the Soviet Union and to shape the growing swell of protest over the treatment of Russia's Jews. The British philosopher Bertrand Russell, an influential friend of the Soviet Union, has repeatedly lent his name to such protests and has himself written to various Soviet spokesmen, including former Premier Khrushchev and Aron Vergelis, the editor of *Sovietish Heimland*. (From his public pronouncements and past history, it is evident that Vergelis serves as a factotum of the Soviet authorities.) In July of 1964 Lord Russell wrote to Vergelis and enclosed an appeal he had received from a Jewish citizen of the USSR. The two letters follow (the second is in translation):[31]

[29] *Pravda*, April 4, 1964.
[30] *London Jewish Chronicle*, April 10, 1964.
[31] Quoted in *Jews in Eastern Europe*, November, 1964. Lord Russell's letter was printed in *Sovietish Heimland;* the appeal of the Russian Jew was not. For the ensuing exchange between Vergelis and Russell, see *Commentary*, January, 1965.

The Editor
Sovietish Heimland
Kirov Street
Moscow, USSR

Dear Sir,

I am writing you to make known the feelings of several Soviet citizens, including members of the Communist Party in the Soviet Union, who have addressed letters to me recently. These Soviet citizens wish to enjoy the right to a full cultural life in the Soviet Union. They are Jews and they feel that they are denied the means of living a complete and satisfying life because they are denied the cultural facilities made available to all other national and minority groups in the USSR. I consider this an important and urgent problem and I should be glad if you would kindly publish the letter I enclose, as well as my own letter.

I write because I am concerned for justice and for the good name of the Soviet Union. Unless people who are concerned for both raise their voices, the cause of peaceful co-existence and the pursuit of peace and general understanding between peoples and nations will be harmed by silence.

Yours sincerely,
Bertrand S. Russell

Moscow, May 20, 1964

Dear Mr. Russell,

The Jews in Russia have read with deep sympathy your letters to N. S. Khrushchev concerning the discrimination of the Jews in the USSR in the trials that deal with economic crimes. But I must say that the people who induced you to do it used your name unexpediently. I believe there was place for a certain tendentiousness in the appreciation of the trials mentioned above. There was no need to use your name for this matter.

In our opinion it is much more important to show to the whole world public-opinion and directly to the leaders of the Soviet Union the problem of enforced assimilation of Jews in the Soviet Union. Indeed, although there are about three million Jews in the USSR, we do not have a newspaper in Moscow, Kiev, Minsk and other centers, there are no Jewish libraries, there are no schools or courses where those who wish it could learn the Jewish language, there are no clubs, theaters or any other center for cultural activity, there is no public organization that could take care especially to serve the Jewish population.

To our deep sorrow it is impossible and even pointless to place this problem before the Soviet government or any other responsible organization.

We want nothing more than to receive the

same rights as the Jews in Poland, Rumania and Czechoslovakia.

We ask you and other influential people to address Premier Khrushchev requesting a solution to this problem. It is urgent.

With respect.

Yours,
(Signature withheld)

All questions concerning our letter we ask you to send to the Jewish journal, *Sovietish Heimland*, Moscow Center, Kirov Street. This letter was written to you on behalf of a great number of people, by a war veteran, an invalid of the war, father of several children, bearer of several war medals, member of the Communist Party.

(Signed)

More recently, Lord Russell has sent a statement voicing his concern over the situation of the Jews in the Soviet Union to the World Union of Jewish Students (February 27, 1966). In this statement he particularly deplored the fact that

Soviet authorities have still taken no steps to end the separation of members of Jewish families disunited in appalling circumstances during the Nazi wars. . . . The one community which suffered the most at the hands of the Nazis—the Jews—has many thousands of individuals in the USSR who have been waiting for more than twenty years to join their close relatives in Israel and other countries.

The general and Jewish press in Western countries has, of course, given coverage to the plight of Russia's Jews, and in recent years a growing number of protests has appeared in the communist press as well. At a rally held in Madison Square Garden in June, 1965, such public figures as Norman Thomas and U. S. Senators Jacob Javits and Robert F. Kennedy voiced their concern over the situation in the Soviet Union. President Johnson has also released statements of concern and received members of groups active in the protest movement, such as the Student Struggle for Soviet Jewry; and a resolution appealing to the Soviet government to grant the Jews of Russia those rights to which they are entitled by law and which are enjoyed by other Soviet nationalities and religious groups has been passed by both chambers of the U. S. Congress. In more recent developments, the Reverend Thurston Davis, S.J., editor of the Jesuit weekly *America*, has urged Catholics to pray for the survival of Jews in the Soviet Union,[32] and representatives of various Jewish organizations, both religious and secular, have issued several formal statements of protest to the

[32] *America*, February 19, 1966.

Moscow government. An Ad Hoc Commission on the Rights of Soviet Jews, chaired by Negro civil-rights leader Bayard Rustin, was convened in New York in March, 1966. The members of the tribunal, which included law experts and Christian religious leaders, heard testimony by eyewitnesses and by authorities on Eastern European affairs. A month later a two-day conference on the status of Soviet Jewry was held in Philadelphia.

It is clear that protests from abroad have had an impact on the internal situation in Russia. The formal disavowal of Kichko's *Judaism without Embellishment* and the easing of restrictions against the baking of matzah were two direct consequences of such protests. Moreover, as the atmosphere within the Soviet Union itself becomes increasingly open and "liberalized," it has become possible to discern among the Soviet intelligentsia a growing sentiment of concern over the enforced "disappearance" of Jews from the annals of Soviet history, both past and present. This concern has been expressed perhaps most vocally by Yevgeni Yevtushenko, the popular young Soviet poet, in "Babi Yar," a poem which first appeared in *Literaturnaya Gazeta*, (Literary Gazette), on September 19, 1961:

There are no memorials at Babi Yar—
The steep slope is the only gravestone.

I am afraid.
Today I am as old as the Jewish people.
It seems to me now that I am a Jew.
And now, crucified on the cross, I die
And even now I bear the marks of the nails.
It seems to me that I am Dreyfus.
The worthy citizenry denounces me and
  judges me.
I am behind prison bars.
I am trapped, hunted, spat upon, reviled
And good ladies in dresses flounced with
  Brussels lace
Shrieking, poke umbrellas in my face.
It seems to me now that I am a boy in
  Byelostok,
Blood flows and spreads across the floor.
Reeking of onion and vodka,
The leading lights of the saloon
Are on the rampage.
Booted aside, I am helpless:
I plead with pogrom thugs
To roars of "Beat the Yids, and save Russia."
A shopkeeper is beating up my mother.
O my Russian people!
You are really international at heart.
But the unclean
Have often loudly taken in vain
Your most pure name.
I know how good is my native land
And how vile it is that, without a quiver
The antisemites styled themselves with pomp
"The union of the Russian people."
It seems to me that I am Anne Frank,

As frail as a twig in April.
And I am full of love
And I have no need of empty phrases.
I want us to look at each other,
How little we can see or smell,
Neither the leaves on the trees nor the sky.
But we can do a lot.
We can tenderly embrace in a dark room.
Someone is coming? Don't be afraid—
It is the noise of spring itself.
Come to me, give me your lips.
Someone is forcing the door.
No, it is the breaking up of the ice. . . .
Wild grasses rustle over Babi Yar.
The trees look down sternly, like judges.
Everything here shrieks silently
And, taking off my cap
I sense that I am turning gray.
And I myself am nothing but a silent shriek,
Over the thousands and thousands buried
  in this place.
I am every old man who was shot here.
I am every boy who was shot here.
No part of me will ever forget any of this.
Let the "Internationale" ring out
When the last anti-Semite on earth is buried.
There is no Jewish blood in mine,
But I am hated by every anti-Semite as a Jew,
And for this reason,
I am a true Russian.[33]

---

[33] Translated by Max Hayward in *Partisan Review*, Winter, 1962. Copyright © by *Partisan Review*, 1962; reprinted by permission.

Following the publication of this poem, Yevtushenko, then 28, was denounced for "over-concern with Jews, for singling out Jews as particular victims of Nazi genocide policy, and for slandering the Soviet people."[34] The poem, however, has remained immensely popular, and at public readings Yevtushenko is compelled by his audiences to read it over and over. The topic is clearly of great interest. Indeed, about a year after "Babi Yar" was first published, the following exchange between Yevtushenko and former Premier Krushchev took place at a meeting between the Soviet leader and several hundred Soviet intellectuals:

Yevtushenko: First of all I want to thank the leaders of the party and government for kindly making it possible for me to speak here. Permit me to begin my speech with a verse which I wrote not so long ago which I consider very timely. [Recites the last two lines of the poem, "Babi Yar."]

Comrade Khrushchev: Comrade Yevtushenko, this poem has no place here.

Yevtushenko: Respected Nikita Sergeevich, I especially selected this poem and with the following purpose in mind. We all know that no one has done more than you in the liquidation of the negative consequen-

[34] Patricia Blake, *Partisan Review*, Winter, 1962. See also her introduction to "New Voices in Russian Writing," a special issue of *Encounter*, April, 1963.

ces of the Stalin cult of personality and we are all very grateful to you for this. However, one problem yet remains which is also a negative consequence of those times, but which today has not yet been resolved. This is the problem of anti-Semitism.

Comrade Khrushchev: That is not a problem.

Yevtushenko: It is a problem, Nikita Sergeevich. It cannot be denied and it cannot be suppressed. It is necessary to come to grips with it time and again. It has a place. I myself was witness to such things. Moreover, it came from people who occupy official posts, and thus it assumed an official character. We cannot go forward to Communism with such a heavy load as Judophobia. And here there can be neither silence nor denial. The problem must be resolved and we hope it will be resolved. The whole progressive world is watching us and the resolution of this problem will even more greatly enhance the authority of our country. By resolution of the problem I mean the cessation of anti-Semitism, along with instituting criminal proceedings against the anti-Semites. This positive measure will give many people of Jewish nationality the opportunity to take heart and will lead us to even greater success in all areas of Communist construction.[35]

[35] See "Russian Art and Anti-Semitism: Two Documents," *Commentary*, December, 1963. This extract reprinted by permission; copyright © 1963 by the American Jewish Committee.

In 1965, the City Council of Kiev announced that it would erect a monument to the "victims of Fascism" at or near Babi Yar, although it is apparent that the unique Jewish tragedy connected with the name of Babi Yar will be glossed over. Nevertheless, the announcement was an indication that the virtual silence which has surrounded the subject of Jewish martyrdom at the hands of the Nazis in World War II may yet be broken. In addition, the Shostakovich Thirteenth Symphony, which contains a choral section setting "Babi Yar" to music, reappeared last year in a gala performance in Moscow. (It had been withdrawn from the repertoire in 1964, after two performances.)

There are a few signs, then, that Soviet policy with regard to the Jews may soon undergo some changes. The editorial which appeared in *Pravda,* containing an explicit condemnation of anti-Semitism (September 5, 1965), followed by two months a remark made by Premier Kosygin during an address to a rally in Riga, Latvia. In the course of his speech Mr. Kosygin denounced "nationalism, great-power chauvinism, racism, and anti-Semitism" as "completely alien to our society and in contradiction to our world view."[36] It was the first such remark made to a home audience in over two decades. But it is highly uncertain whether statements like these mark

[36] *Pravda,* July 19, 1965.

the beginnings of a real educational effort to
eliminate the manifestations of anti-Semitism.
In late October, 1965, the Soviet Union effectively blocked a draft article, proposed by
the United States and Brazil, to be inserted
into the United Nations "Convention on the
Elimination of All Forms of Racial Discrimination." The proposal was meant to "con-
demn anti-Semitism and take appropriate actions for its eradication." The Soviet delegation, by suggesting an impossible amendment
to this proposal, forced the committee to pass
a resolution doing away with all references
to specific forms of race hatred. The proposed
Soviet amendment read as follows:

> States Parties condemn anti-Semitism, Zion-
> ism, Nazism, neo-Nazism and all other forms
> of the policy and ideology of colonialism,
> national and race hatred and exclusiveness,
> and shall take action as appropriate for the
> speedy eradication of those misanthropic
> [subsequently changed to "inhuman"] ideas
> and practices in the territories subject to their
> jurisdiction.[37]

Despite such periodic reversals, the situation

[37] See "Soviet Jewry: A Current Survey," A Commission
Study presented at the Ad Hoc Commission on the Rights
of Soviet Jews, March 18, 1966. At a subsequent session
(Spring, 1966) of the United Nations Commission on
Human Rights, the article condemning anti-Semitism was
finally approved and adopted. The Soviet Union ab-
stained from voting.

does seem to be improving somewhat, if with agonizing slowness. One cannot, however, predict in confidence a steady process of amelioration: On August 16, 1966, it was learned that economic trials had begun once again, and that at least one Soviet Jew had been sentenced to death for alleged economic crimes. Yet it does seem that the Soviet Union is becoming somewhat more responsive to pressures from abroad and to the weight of public opinion at home, even though such events as the recent trial and conviction of the authors Andrei Sinyavsky and Yuli Daniel reflect, at best, an ambiguous attitude toward the process of liberalization. The same *Pravda* editorial which condemned anti-Semitism, in the words of Lenin, as a "foul fanning of racial specialness and national enmity," contained a paragraph which, one may hope, could some day serve to fashion Soviet policy toward the Jews:

It must not be forgotten that the people of the whole world, and particularly the people who have freed themselves from imperialist oppression, look upon the Soviet Union, the world's first country of socialism, and on the relations that have taken shape among the peoples of our country, as a model. This means that strengthening the fraternal friendship among the people of the USSR is a most important international obligation of each Soviet Republic.

Suggested Readings

(See footnotes to Historical Afterword
for additional references)

Baron, Salo, *The Russian Jew under the Tsars and Soviets*, 1963. An historical survey.

Decter, Moshe, "The Status of the Jews in the Soviet Union," *Foreign Affairs*, January, 1963. Basic. For a Soviet rejoinder see S. Rozin, "I Speak as a Soviet Jew," *The Minority of One*, May, 1963. Decter's reply appeared in *The Minority of One*, July, 1963.

——, "The Lvov Case: A Self-Portrait of Soviet Anti-Semitism," *Midstream*, June, 1963.

——, "The Soviet Book That Shook the Communist World," *Midstream*, June, 1964.

——, "Soviet Justice and the Jews: Three Case Histories," *Midstream*, March, 1965.

Friedberg, Maurice, "The State of Soviet Jewry,"

Commentary, January, 1965. Excellent summary.

Goldberg, B. Z., *The Jewish Problem in the Soviet Union*, 1961. Highly personal and apologetic.

Hindus, Maurice, *House without a Roof*, 1961. Readable, illuminating.

Jews in Eastern Europe, a periodical survey of events affecting Jews in the Soviet Bloc. Contains much vital information and fair translations of pertinent documents.

Kolarz, W., "The Secularization of Soviet Jewry," in *Religion in the Soviet Union*, 1962.

Korey, William, "The Legal Position of the Jews in the Soviet Union," *Midstream*, May, 1966. Good survey.

Leneman, L., *La Tragédie des Juifs en URSS*, 1959. Especially good on the purges of Jewish writers.

The New Leader, September 14, 1959. A special documentary issue on Jews in the Soviet Union.

Parkes, James, "Anti-Semitism in the Soviet Union," in *Anti-Semitism*, 1963. By a leading scholar of Jewish-Christian relations.

Salisbury, Harrison, "The Rise of Anti-Semitism," in *A New Russia?*, 1963. Personal observations by an informed writer.

Schechtman, Joseph, *Star in Eclipse; Russian Jewry Revisited*, 1961. Tendentious.

Schwarz, S., *Jews in the Soviet Union*, 1951. Authoritative and well-documented study.

Teller, Judd, *The Kremlin, the Jews and the Middle East*, 1957. Solid, readable.

Other **SIGNET** Books of Current Interest

☐ **THE PRISONERS OF QUAI DONG by Victor Kolpacoff.** More than the standard war novel, this highly acclaimed book causes us to consider our own motives in relation to what we are doing to ourselves. "The most impressive first novel in a very long time."—**Newsweek**
(#T3500—75¢)

☐ **THE ARMIES OF THE NIGHT by Norman Mailer.** The Pulitzer-Prize winning chronicle of the three days of anti-Vietnam demonstrations in Washington during October 1967 by the bestselling author of **The Naked and the Dead.** "Brilliant writing, brilliant reportage."—**Chicago Sun-Times.**
(#Y3712—$1.25)

☐ **HOW TO GET OUT OF VIETNAM: A workable solution to the Worst Problem of Our Time by John Kenneth Galbraith.** The distinguished economist, political theorist, and bestselling author offers a practical plan for U.S. withdrawal from "a war we cannot win, should not wish to win, are not winning and which our people do not support."
(#C3414—35¢)

☐ **BACKGROUND TO VIETNAM by Bernard Newman.** A highly qualified observer's unbiased account of Vietnam: its history, its people, its politics, and its leaders. "A book full of information which reads like a story and raises all the important questions."—**Harper's**

More SIGNET Books of Current Interest

☐ **AMERICA VS. AMERICA: The Revolution in Middle-Class Values by James A. Michener.** Written out of concern for the rebellion of the younger generation against the values of their parents, this Broadside explores present middle-class guidelines and the contradictions between what many Americans say they believe and what they actually do. (#P3819—60¢)

☐ **MIAMI AND THE SIEGE OF CHICAGO: An Informal History of the Republican and Democratic Conventions of 1968 by Norman Mailer.** From the pen of "the best writer in America" **(Book Week),** comes a unique and deeply moving report of the shame of Miami and the shambles of Chicago during the 1968 presidential conventions. (#Q3785—95¢)

☐ **FREE TO LIVE, FREE TO DIE by Malcolm Boyd.** A collection of meditations on current subjects in the hard-hitting, free-swinging, contemporary slang of "the coffeehouse priest." By the author of the bestseller, **Are You Running With Me, Jesus?** (#T3426—75¢)

☐ **VIOLENCE: AMERICA IN THE SIXTIES by Arthur Schlesinger, Jr.** In this sobering look at the present era of violence, Mr. Schlesinger probes the failure of the intellectual community to produce sustained, national self-examination after the assassination of our leaders. (#D3747—50¢)